A Moment *for* Mom

EVERYDAY DEVOTIONS & PRAYERS

EDITORS *of* GUIDEPOSTS

A Moment for Mom

Published by Guideposts
100 Reserve Road, Suite E200
Danbury, CT 06810
Guideposts.org

Acknowledgments

Every attempt has been made to credit the sources of copyrighted material used in this book. If any such acknowledgment has been inadvertently omitted or miscredited, receipt of such information would be appreciated.

Scripture quotations marked (ESV) are taken from *The Holy Bible, English Standard Version.* Copyright © 2001 by Crossway Bibles, a division of Good News Publishers. Used by permission. All rights reserved.

Scripture quotations marked (MSG) are taken from *The Message.* Copyright © 1993, 2002, 2018 by Eugene H. Peterson.

Scripture quotations marked (NASB) are taken from the *New American Standard Bible®,* Copyright © 1960, 1971, 1977, 1995, 2020 by The Lockman Foundation. All rights reserved.

Scripture quotations marked (NIV) are taken from *The Holy Bible, New International Version®, NIV®.* Copyright © 1973, 1978, 1984, 2011 by Biblica, Inc. Used by permission. All rights reserved worldwide.

Scripture quotations marked (NKJV) are taken from the *New King James Version®.* Copyright © 1982 by Thomas Nelson. Used by permission. All rights reserved.

Scripture quotations marked (NLT) are taken from the *Holy Bible, New Living Translation.* Copyright © 1996, 2004, 2007, 2015 by Tyndale House Foundation. Used by permission of Tyndale House Publishers Inc., Carol Stream, Illinois. All rights reserved.

Cover and interior design by Serena Fox Design
Typeset by Aptara, Inc.

Special thanks to Amanda Ericson, Sabra Ciancanelli, Stephanie Reeves, and Val Chiofalo.

ISBN 978-1-961126-78-7 (softcover)
ISBN 978-1-961126-79-4 (epub)

Printed and bound in the United States of America

This book is intended to be a spiritual reference volume only, not a medical manual. The presented information is meant to help you make informed decisions about your physical, emotional, and spiritual health. It is not intended to be a substitute for any treatment prescribed by your doctor. If you are experiencing symptoms or suspect that you have a medical problem, please seek medical help.

"*Motherhood tells us everything we need to know about faith. Being a parent teaches us in the clearest terms how God, our Father in heaven, relates to us. His love, His frustrations, His compassion for us... The way we feel about our kids is about as close as we can get to grasping how God feels about us, His children.*"

Savannah Guthrie

Contents

Introduction 4

Precious New Life 6

Struggling Child 7

A Gentle Answer 8

Finding Stillness 9

Feeding on Faithfulness . . 10

Depend on God 11

Give Up Control 12

God's Guidance 13

Part of God's
    Perfect Plan 14

Motherhood: A Worldwide
    Sisterhood 15

Blessed Rest 16

In His Hands 17

At This Moment 18

Make New Mistakes 19

The Quail's Gift 20

The Power of Belief 21

Passion and Purpose 22

Miracles Abound 23

Relinquish the Struggle . . . 24

The Dog Training
    Lesson 25

Taking It All In 26

Open Our Hearts 27

Rhythms of Grace 28

Have Fun 29

Napping? Never! 30

My Refuge 31

Blessed Interruptions 32

The Lighter Side 33

You Are Stronger
    Than You Think 34

Releasing a Child
    into God's Calling—
    Notes from a
    Missionary Mom 35

Handover 36

Bless Others 37

Your Fresh Start 38

Courage 39

Teach Us to Pray 40

Words to Live By 41

Prune Your Priorities 42

Now Is the Time 43

Rejoice 44

God's Got This 45

Not Alone 46

Rejecting Insecurity 47

Comparison and
  Competition 48

He Is with You 49

A Sacred No 50

Perfectly Imperfect 51

A Change of Heart. 52

God's Gift of
  Forgiveness 53

Keep Dreaming 54

Nurturing a Habit
  of Prayer through
  Visual Cues 55

All in God's Time 56

God of Order 57

Anxiety Abated 58

Positivity Ahead 59

Pick Up Sticks 60

God of Second Chances . . . 61

God Is Love 62

Heavenly Light 63

Divinely Led 64

Game Night 65

Make the Most of
  Your Time 66

A Habit of Gratitude 67

Plant Yourself in
  God's Word 68

Answered Prayers 69

Exchanging Burdens
  for Blessings 70

Follow the Good
  Shepherd 71

Embrace the New 72

Do Away with Doubt 73

An Open Door 74

More Than One
  Way to Be a Mom 75

True Value 76

Seasons of Change 77

Your Prayers 78

The Wisdom of Not
  Knowing 79

A Nature Trail to the
  Gospel Message 80

Behold 81

Progress, Not Perfection . . . 82

Angels Watching Over . . . 83

Gratitude in Your Heart . . . 84

Imaginative Prayer 85

Grow in Christ 86

When to Say No 87

Build Sandcastles 88

Time to Rest 89

The Mentoring Spirit
of Motherhood 90

When God Seems Silent . . . 91

An Extra Hour 92

Are You Joyful? 93

The Hardest Part 94

Exercise Your
Prayer Life 95

God Doesn't Make
Mistakes. 96

Patience. 97

Life's Curves 98

Overflowing Blessings 99

Prayer Walks 100

God Will Rescue You 101

Love First 102

Practice Stillness 103

Let the Spirit Lead 104

Helping Our Children
Renew and Rewire
Their Minds 105

Your Divine Journey 106

Good Change Ahead 107

Waiting 108

God Will Hold
Your Hand 109

What Really Matters 110

Your Life Is His
Masterpiece 111

Clear the Air. 112

Calm Your Nerves 113

Time to Listen 114

The Unique Role of
a Mother-in-Law 115

Banish Self-Doubt 116

God Is Always Faithful . . . 117

Childlike Faith 118

Change and Resiliency . . . 119

Tiny Tendrils. 120

Stargazing. 121

Forgiving Yourself 122

Take Care 123

Courage and Strength. . . . 124

Modeling a More
Positive Perspective . . . 125

Little Things 126

God's Perfect Love 127

Hope 128

Worldly Problems 129

Mothers of the Bible 131

Our Contributors 134

Entries by Theme. 138

A Note from the Editors. . . 139

Introduction

Dear children, let us not love with words or speech
but with actions and in truth.
1 John 3:18 (NIV)

Mothers everywhere know what it means to love in their actions and their truth. Mothering is the best, toughest, most meaningful, most exasperating, most joyous undertaking of our lives. There's always something to follow up on or plan—not to mention do—for the family.

Fortunately, there's a Helper ready to step in—and that is God. He sees and appreciates everything that mothers (and those who take on mothering roles) do, big and small, and the Bible tells us about God's great esteem for mothers. For example, He is compared to a comforting mother in Isaiah 66:13. Proverbs 31:28 (NIV) lauds the qualities of a mother of action, whose "children arise and call her blessed."

The creation story of Genesis gives us our first mother, Eve, and both the Old and New Testaments show us God's tender care of mothers, but God's love for us, the mothers of the world, expands infinitely beyond the Bible.

God embraces mothers. When we are buoyant with joy, He hears us sing out our praise and thanks to Him. When we face trials and painful uncertainties, He heeds our pleas and sends His angels to sustain us. Through it all, He is love.

The devotional pages in *A Moment for Mom: Everyday Devotions and Prayers* include a related Bible verse, as well as a reflection and a prayer—written for a mother's heart and needs. Full of encouragement, biblical advice, and comfort, each page is offered in the hopes that it may help illuminate your own steps toward tranquility and spiritual nourishment.

Reflections and prayers cover such topics as faith, strength, trust, and wisdom. If you find yourself short on time—and *everyone* does—you can turn to the Entries by Theme on page 138 at the back of the book, where keywords will point you to entries that fit your current need. For times that are especially brief, we suggest that you go directly to the prayer on the page and, perhaps, read it aloud. We hope that this moment of connection with the Lord will be sweet and fulfilling for you.

Sprinkled throughout the book are one-page essays and articles by a group of beloved Guideposts writers who are moms. Their chorus of varied voices brings you their experiences with motherhood and prayer, offering amusing anecdotes, helpful suggestions, and true stories of lessons learned. You might be surprised how their insights resonate with your heart.

By picking up this book, you are stepping forward on a path toward hopeful introspection and connection with God. But you'll find that the benefits ripple out far beyond you. Every few minutes you take to nurture yourself will give you the tools to better nurture the family depending on you. As we instruct and love our children, we do what God bids us to do, as He intended from the beginning.

The gifts of God sustain us, and in turn, we do so much to sustain the people who depend on us. But we must never forget that there is Someone who loves us infinitely and wants us to reflect some of that caring attention and intention back upon ourselves. We are mothers, but we are also the children of God, walking in love. —Lisa Guernsey

As you have heard from the beginning, his command is that you walk in love.
—2 John 1:6 (NIV)

Precious New Life

Yet you brought me out of the womb; you made me trust
in you, even at my mother's breast. From birth I was cast
on you; from my mother's womb you have been my God.
Psalm 22:9–10 (NIV)

Take a moment to think about how much God truly loves you.
Then consider that you need to be parented yourself. Who
better to do that than our perfect Father? Can you admit your
own neediness and ask God to help you accept His abiding
love and acceptance? When you bask in God's sweet care, you
cannot help but be a better parent.

DEAR LORD, THANK YOU FOR THE GIFT of precious
new life. You are an awesome Creator! I lift up to You today
the new babies You have brought into my life.

Help me to trust You with every detail of every day. In
that trust, I will rest and be at peace. Help me to ask for help
when I need it. I'm not meant to do this alone. I need You,
and I need others.

I pray all new babies will sense how much they are
loved—just as I need to sense how much I am loved—and
that this love becomes a source of peace for all of us. Help
me not to be constantly worried but to enjoy my days as
much as I can and trust You with each new challenge. In
Jesus's name, amen.

Struggling Child

Not only that, but we rejoice in our sufferings, knowing that suffering produces endurance, and endurance produces character, and character produces hope, and hope does not put us to shame, because God's love has been poured into our hearts through the Holy Spirit who has been given to us.

Romans 5:3–5 (ESV)

It's hard to watch our children suffer! But whatever trial, loss, or temptation they are going through, Jesus knows. There is nothing too hard, painful, or devastating for Him to identify with. When we bring our suffering to Him in prayer, He feels our pain as we feel His comfort. This is true for you as well as for your children.

DEAR GOD, THANK YOU for my children. I am so grateful for the gift they are. You know that I want to fix things for them when they struggle. I want to smooth it all over so that I can see them joyful again. But, Lord, I know that they need to find their own way.

Help me remind them of both my love for them and Yours. When they wrestle with problems, give them wisdom and peace in their situations. Help them understand their need for You. Help them to trust You. Give us all patience in the process.

Guard their hearts and their minds, Lord, so that they won't listen to voices telling them to take shortcuts or to give up hope. I place my struggling child in Your hands. They are Yours. It's in Jesus's name that I pray, amen.

A Gentle Answer

A gentle answer turns away wrath,
but a harsh word stirs up anger.

Proverbs 15:1 (NIV)

No matter how hard we try to set our hearts against speaking harshly to our children, sometimes their behavior elicits ire. Instead of lashing out in anger, try asking yourself a few questions. Is this problem or infraction as serious as you are making it? Is what you are tempted to say only going to demonstrate your anger? What can you say that could instruct your child or correct the situation? Are you modeling compassionate behavior?

LORD, YOUR WORD SAYS to treat others the way we want to be treated. Then why is it so hard for me to speak to my children the way I want to be spoken to? Guard my mouth, Lord. And guard my heart, because Your Word also says that from the overflow of the heart, the mouth speaks.

Help me to show my children the patience and grace You have shown to me. Help me to see that they are learning about life and relationships just as I am. It's Your kindness that is meant to lead us to repentance, and it will be my kindness that teaches my children and binds us closer together in love. In Jesus's name I pray, amen.

Finding Stillness

Be still before the LORD and wait patiently for him.
Psalm 37:7 (NIV)

We know that being still is an important part of our spiritual growth, but it's difficult to find the time for stillness and harder yet to wait patiently for God's answers. In those small moments when you can be still, open your heart and allow yourself to experience God's grace, letting His presence fill you. The quality of this time is far more important than the quantity.

DEAR LORD, THANK YOU for the gift of quiet. It's not easy to find tranquility as a mom, but I know it's important. I want to hear Your voice, and I can only do that when I'm still and listening. Just as I want to teach my kids to wait for the things they want to have or do, I need to learn this lesson too.

You are a good Father. You are always on time with Your provision. Thank You for guiding me on how to parent. Thank You for the moments of quiet You set apart for me. Help me to take hold of them. In Jesus's name I pray, amen.

Feeding on Faithfulness

by Eryn Lynum

As a mother, I have always found courage in Psalm 37:5 (ESV): "Commit your way to the LORD; trust in him and he will act." At the same time, I often struggle if I cannot see or sense God doing His part in acting on behalf of my family. I question whether I trust Him enough or if my faith is feeble. Yet He has given me perspective by narrowing my focus on the preceding verses.

Based on Psalm 37:5, I began praying in my own words, *Lord, in the nitty-gritty, messy middle ground of these motherhood days, help me to delight in You.*

Yet this, too, felt forced at times. I want joy and delight to naturally bubble up, like when my children shake a can of carbonated water before popping it open. But if I'm honest, my delight more closely resembles the fizzy water after a child leaves it out on the counter overnight—flat.

I didn't understand this passage's power until God drew my attention to Psalm 37:3 (NKJV): "Trust in the LORD, and do good; dwell in the land, and feed on His faithfulness."

Am I feeding on His faithfulness?

The Hebrew word interpreted as "feed on" has strong shepherding connotations. It gives a rich picture of grazing in a safe pasture with abundant provision. This reminded me of Psalm 23:1–2 (NIV), "The LORD is my shepherd, I lack nothing. He makes me lie down in green pastures...."

My tendency has been to force my faith—to commit diligently enough, trust deep enough, and delight authentically enough. Now I'm discovering God's gentle invitation to feed on His faithfulness as I watch Him work mightily in my home.

Depend on God

For we walk by faith, not by sight.

2 Corinthians 5:7 (NKJV)

When things look dark or you are uncertain of the best course of action, instead of relying on your perception of the situation, turn to prayer. God has perfect vision. Trust that He has everything under control.

LORD, I REALLY WANT TO TRUST You. You have always been faithful, and You always will be faithful. Even when I can't see it, You are at work for my good and Your glory. If I could see everything You're doing, I wouldn't need faith; I would have sight. So, like the father beseeching Jesus to heal his child, I cry out, "I believe, Lord. Help my unbelief!"

You see the beginning, the middle, and the end of all my circumstances. Help me to trust that You are in control when I most definitely am not. You are a good God who cares deeply for me and my family. I trust You, Lord. Amen.

Give Up Control

The king's heart is a stream of water in the hand
of the L<small>ORD</small>; he turns it wherever he will.
Proverbs 21:1 (ESV)

Some things in life are simply beyond our control. As much as we might want something, we can't always make it happen. We can do our part, but ultimately there are times when we must adopt a "wait and see" approach. Letting life unfold by releasing the outcome to God is a gift we can give ourselves.

DEAR GOD, MORE OFTEN THAN not, as a mom, I feel out of control. When my children are not with me, I don't know what they're doing, and I have to entrust them to You. Remind me constantly that You're the best one to be in control. When I release my grip, my hands are free to accept Your good gifts.

Your Word says that I can't add one day to my life by worrying. That's so true! In fact, I probably take years off my life with stress when I try to take control. I can make my plans, Lord, and that's not a bad thing, but please help me to release those plans into Your hands to do what is best. Thank You for being in control. I relax my grip in the name of Jesus, amen.

God's Guidance

Direct my footsteps according to your word;
let no sin rule over me.
Psalm 119:133 (NIV)

God has given us boundaries and guidelines to ease our life's journey. We understand that when we stay on His path, we have purpose and direction. Sometimes your children may feel that boundaries are limiting their freedom. When this happens, urge them to shift their perspective to look at boundaries as guiding them to victory. They will find the idea of triumph much more appealing than restriction.

FATHER GOD, BOUNDARIES WERE Your idea. I know this because from the beginning of Creation, You told the oceans they could only come so far. If there wasn't a shore, everything would be underwater! Without boundaries like these and those in our human societies, there would be chaos.

So I ask You for wisdom. Help me teach my kids how guardrails keep us safe and that rules help us enjoy our freedom. But help me also to show great grace when rules are broken or boundaries are breached.

Jesus, You came that we might have life abundantly! Help me know how to guide my children in this truth. It's in Your name that I pray, amen.

Part of God's Perfect Plan

*I praise you because I am fearfully and wonderfully
made; your works are wonderful, I know that full well.*

Psalm 139:14 (NIV)

You are wonderfully made! Let this verse come to your mind
the next time you feel as if you aren't good enough. You are
loved by God. Release yourself from negative thinking—
wishing you were different, better at this or that—and rest in
the beautiful fact that God gave you special gifts and unique
experiences to share with the world.

LORD, SOMETIMES I WONDER what I'm made for. I
know being a mom is important, and I love my kids fiercely,
so I thank You for the purpose of raising them. Would You
show me what other gifts and abilities You have given me?

I want to have the right priorities. I want to be the person
You have made me to be. I want to love my family well, and I
want to glorify You in all that I do.

Help me to see myself as You see me. Remind me day by
day of who I am in You. It's in Jesus's name that I pray, amen.

Motherhood: A Worldwide Sisterhood

by Jeannie Blackmer

I had the privilege to visit mom groups throughout Guatemala connected to a ministry I work with: The MomCo by MOPS International. We visited groups in poverty-stricken areas where gang violence and abuse against women run rampant.

We visited a shelter for young moms who had escaped abusive husbands. This program takes five women with their children for 9 months and provides food, shelter, clothing, counseling, and training in skills such as sewing, baking, and jewelry making. After the women graduate, the ministry provides them with a furnished home to live in. It connects them to a local church, gives them some seed money to restart their lives, and schedules visits for the next few months to encourage them.

We were visiting the night before a group of women launched into their new lives. Each woman shared a bit of her story. I was struck by how closely we are all connected, even though we live in different parts of the world. My own mom escaped an abusive husband and gave my siblings a new life in a safe environment. She then met my dad and put her old life behind her. As these women were about to do.

As we prayed together with an interpreter, so many of our prayers echoed each other's. We prayed about our thankfulness for new beginnings and our fear for our children's safety. We asked for authentic friendships and healthy relationships, and for the strength to be the moms our children needed. After prayers we shared chocolate, tears, laughter, and hugs.

Moms—no matter where we live, what our socioeconomic situation may be, or what languages we speak—are connected. Truly motherhood is a sisterhood everywhere and forever.

Blessed Rest

And on the seventh day God ended His work which
He had done, and He rested on the seventh day from
all His work which He had done.
Genesis 2:2 (NKJV)

Do you find that sometimes you are too busy to even think?
You know that rest is necessary and important, but as a mother,
you often sacrifice your rest for the sake of others' needs. When
you can, give yourself permission to take time off, to say no to
things you don't want to do, and to find time—even little bits of
it—to relax and restore your soul.

DEAR GOD, I'M TIRED. There's always more to do. Something's got to give, and I don't want it to be my family's mental health. Teach me more of what soul rest really looks like. I know I need to rest my body, but if my soul is in turmoil, even physical rest doesn't help.

Teach me to guard my days and remind me I don't have to schedule every minute. Help me place a high value on family time. Eliminate my people-pleasing ways; You're the only one I need to please. Give me the wisdom to find tools to help me organize my days, and the strength to say no when I need to. Thank You for loving me without my doing anything to earn it. Amen.

In His Hands

He appointed the moon for seasons;
The sun knows its going down.
Psalm 104:19 (NKJV)

God holds the entire universe together. He is the caretaker of the world. When you feel like you are at your wit's end managing all that you are responsible for—when supporting your family, friends, and so many others seems as overwhelming as runaway stagecoach horses in old Western movies—take a deep breath. Imagine yourself passing the reins to the One in power. He has it all under control.

LORD, I HAVE SO MANY PLATES spinning, I'm afraid one of these days they're all just going to crash to the ground. Help me to release those things that I really don't have to carry on my own. Help me take a step back, breathe deeply, and let You take control. Help me understand deep down in my soul that I am enough.

Please nudge me hard when I'm taking on too much. Before I sign up for anything, remind me to reevaluate and ask if it's something that really needs to happen. Thank You for Your gentle correction in my life. I love You. Amen.

At This Moment

Why, you do not even know what will happen tomorrow.
What is your life? You are a mist that appears for a
little while and then vanishes.

James 4:14 (NIV)

Planning and preparation are a necessary function of being a mother. Still, we need to remind ourselves that when we focus too closely on tomorrow, we lose the gift of the present moment. If you find yourself overly concerned with the future, ask God: *What can I do right now—at this very moment—to align myself with Your plan?* Then quiet your mind and listen for God's answer.

DEAR LORD, TODAY HAS ENOUGH worries of its own, right? But it's so hard to draw the line between planning and obsessing about what will happen tomorrow. Help me be present. Help me hold my plans loosely. If a friend or family member is upset, help me to stop, sit with them, and hear their heart. If plans need to be scrapped to make room for cherishing this moment, help me be okay with that.

Today can hold so much beauty, Father God. Help me not to miss it in my desire to have my tomorrows all planned out. Amen.

Make New Mistakes

But those who hope in the LORD will renew their strength.
They will soar on wings like eagles; they will run and not
grow weary, they will walk and not be faint.
Isaiah 40:31 (NIV)

The landscape of motherhood is littered with *shouldas, couldas,*
and *wouldas.* At best, our mistakes are small and even humor-
ous. It's easy to become crippled by the fear of making mistakes. We do our best when we learn from our errors instead
of repeating them. Endeavor to develop a healthy acceptance
that trial and error is a part of life and learning. When we
realize that God is the Creator—the Whisperer of new ideas,
new ways, and improvements—we can begin to let go of
self-judgment and allow ourselves to make new mistakes.

LORD, REMIND ME THAT WHEN my children were
learning to walk, I didn't reprimand them when they fell
down. Life is a learning process. Thank You for the grace You
always offer to me; help me to offer it to myself too.

Oh, if only I could see myself as You see me! You love me
no matter how much I fail. I will inevitably fail if I'm going
to grow in my skills, my relationships, my parenting. But
love covers a multitude of sins. I am grateful. In Jesus's name,
amen.

The Quail's Gift
by Courtney Ellis

A few years ago, I became an avid birdwatcher (a *birder*, as we call ourselves). Though I'm hard-pressed to choose a favorite species—a difficult task in a world buzzing with hummingbirds and flamingos, peacocks and albatrosses—I have a real soft spot for the California quail. Whether or not you live in the Southwest, you may have seen a California quail. Walt Disney featured them in his movie *Bambi*. These wonderful, plump little ground-dwelling birds with their speckled brown feathers and funny waddling gait are delightfully cinematic.

Why do I love quail? Because they've taught me so much about motherhood. Many birds are doting parents, mated pairs bringing food back to the nest in a flurry of wings and exhaustion. (Baby birds are *hungry*!) But quails make this task a little bit easier. Quails nest *communally*. These birds share the duties of feeding, caregiving, and watching for predators, turning the arduous task of raising their young into a group project. What genius!

The most difficult days of mothering for me are nearly always those I spend in isolation. I'm naturally introverted, so it can be hard for me to reach out and ask for help. But whenever I hesitate, I think of the quail. A single quail won't make it far. These birds nest on the ground and are easy prey. Quail fledglings are ravenous—a mother trying to feed them on her own would soon be overwhelmed. Sharing the burden with other birds is key.

Today I mother alongside a community of friends who have become like family. We lean on one another, sharing meals and carpooling and benefiting from the wisdom God grows within each of us. We are stronger—and happier—together.

The Power of Belief

They replied, "Believe in the Lord Jesus, and
you will be saved—you and your household."
Acts 16:31 (NIV)

Every day, we trust and have faith in things we cannot see.
Our very beliefs determine the world we choose to live in.
As Dr. Norman Vincent Peale famously said, "Change your
thoughts and you change your world." What are you thinking
about?

LORD, SOMETIMES I JUST WANT to see You face-to-face.
I want to sit across a table from You and share my heart. I
believe I will do that for eternity, but right now I need to
believe. When the world would tell me I'm on my own to figure things out, remind me of Your Word that says You have
a plan for me. You have always kept Your promises, so when
You say that You will never leave me or forsake me, help me
to take You at Your word. Remind me of the myriad of ways
You reveal Yourself in my life. I do believe, Lord. Please help
me when my belief wobbles. In Jesus's name, amen.

Passion and Purpose

When he came and saw the grace of God, he was glad,
and he exhorted them all to remain faithful to the
Lord with steadfast purpose.
Acts 11:23 (ESV)

Jesus gave you passion and the ability to have purpose in your
life. When you are feeling lost, turn to the things you are passionate about. What activities make your spirit soar? Ask God to
help you make the most of the specific talents He has given you.

LORD, I AM NOT LIKE anyone else. I am uniquely me.
Help me not to compare myself to anyone but the person
staring back at me in the mirror. I know You have given me
gifts and abilities. I want to use them for Your glory.

Help me reveal things about myself I may have kept hidden for years because of unkind words from others. Give me
the courage to use my gifts to bless others. No matter how
insignificant I may think those gifts are, in Your hands they
are multiplied. Convince me of my worth as I pursue my
passions for Your name's sake. Amen.

Miracles Abound

Jesus did many other things as well. If every one of them were written down, I suppose that even the whole world would not have room for the books that would be written.

John 21:25 (NIV)

God's miracles—large and small—happen all the time. Meaningful moments of God's presence grace each day, and mothers often bear witness, perhaps with more frequency than any other group. John wrote that the Bible contains only a fraction of the many amazing things Jesus did. Add to that the number of miracles that have taken place since His time on Earth. Astounding! If you can, take a moment and think about how many of these divine wonders you have witnessed.

FATHER, FROM THE MIRACLE of birth to the healing of a friend with an aggressive form of cancer, You have shown Your power. You are the same yesterday, today, and forever, so Your miracles continue today. Thank You for the big and little ways You reveal Yourself every day.

The stars light up the night sky. A friend I've been thinking about calls me out of the blue. When we thought there was no hope for our situation, an answer suddenly appears. Coincidence? No. Your hand is evident in it all. Let me not take for granted all You do every day. It's in the matchless name of Jesus that I pray, amen.

Relinquish the Struggle

The flowers appear on the earth, the time of singing has
come, and the voice of the turtledove is heard in our land.
Song of Solomon 2:12 (ESV)

Wildflowers grow and flourish under God's care. This is a
beautiful reminder that even when life seems overwhelming,
there is no need to struggle—God will take care of you. In this
moment, what struggles can you place in His care? As you
pray, give Him those difficulties and ask Him to fill you with
His peace.

DEAR GOD, SOMETIMES WHEN I consider all that it
takes to keep my world going, I have moments of doubt that
You can handle it all. Forgive me for trying to do Your job
for You. Take my little fingers, one by one, and pry them off
those things I'm grasping. You have given me stewardship
over a lot of things, but they still belong to You.

All my joys, all my struggles, all my dreams, they're all
Yours. I release them, Lord. Help me not to grab them back
again. You know what is best for me. I have tunnel vision,
but You see all of eternity. Thank You for Your care for me.
It's in Jesus's name that I pray, amen.

The Dog Training Lesson

by Peggy Frezon

Our golden retriever Sophie stood beside me in the training class, her blond, fluffy tail wagging, waiting patiently for the next direction. My eight-year-old granddaughter, Grace, a budding future veterinarian, attended the classes with us and watched with interest.

"Ask your dog to sit," the instructor said. "Always use a pleasant tone of voice. Why would a dog want to obey if you were harsh?" We learned to train our dogs through repetition, gentleness, and rewards, such as pats, hugs, and especially treats. "Positive training methods guide the dog with compassion, and this helps create strong bonds between you and your dog," the instructor added.

"Sit," I said gently, careful not to tug the leash. Sophie sat. "Good girl!" I told her and handed her a cookie.

That weekend, I was in the kitchen, watching Grace play a board game with her sister. My younger granddaughter was not in the mood to cooperate. Sometimes Grace, the older sibling, could be bossy and demanding. But this time I heard her speak gently and kindly, guiding her sister to play by the rules.

"You two are getting along together very nicely," I said. "I like to see that."

"Of course we are, Grandma," Grace said. "I only use positive methods."

Here I thought my granddaughter had been attending classes with me to learn about dog obedience, but she was really learning something more. She was applying what she observed in class to her own relationships. It reminded me that our young ones are always observing our behaviors.

I smiled and held out a plate. "Now, how about a cookie?"

Taking It All In

When they had seen him, they spread the word concerning
what had been told them about this child, and all who heard
it were amazed at what the shepherds said to them. But Mary
treasured up all these things and pondered them in her heart.

Luke 2:17–19 (NIV)

In the above verse, Mary is observed taking in the miracle
and storing up the memories of Jesus's birth and all that trans-
pired concerning it. How can you be sure to follow her lead
and "treasure up" all the special moments with the children in
your life? Like Mary, you simply pause and ponder them in your
heart.

LORD, I DON'T WANT TO MISS what You're doing in the
lives of my children. Help me be mindful and present. Help
me not to race madly from one activity to another and forget
to savor the sweet moments I have with them. Help us all to
slow down. Remind me to mark the significant moments in
their lives—all the firsts, the triumphs, and the defeats. I will
treasure these things in my heart. But I also want to treasure
my children as people. Help me to know their hearts, to ask
questions, and to really listen to them. I am so grateful for
the gift of my kids. Thank You for the privilege of being their
mom. In Jesus's name, amen.

Open Our Hearts

For from his fullness we have all received, grace upon
grace. For the law was given through Moses;
grace and truth came through Jesus Christ.
John 1:16–17 (ESV)

Sometimes we make the mistake of freezing people—
especially our children—in time. We witness their worst moments and lock them into those moments, bestowing on them
a negative trait as something they own. We lose faith that they
can change. When we recognize this, we can pray for Christ to
lead us to let go of our assumptions about our children and
open our hearts to see them as He sees them. With our help
and Christ's grace, children overcome negative behaviors and
change.

HEAVENLY FATHER, JUST AS I HAVE received grace
upon grace through Jesus, help me to give grace upon grace
to my kids—and others I may judge wrongly simply by their
behavior. Help me to be a kind shepherd who leads my flock
but will leave the ninety-nine to find the one who has wandered. I imagine a shepherd being frantic at the loss of his
sheep, not angry that they wandered away. Give me a heart
of love and grace. I want to be seen not for the things I've
done wrong but for the potential in me. That's how You treat
me. Help me to treat others the same. In Jesus's name, amen.

Rhythms of Grace

"I'll show you how to take a real rest. Walk with me and
work with me—watch how I do it. Learn the
unforced rhythms of grace."

Matthew 11:28 (MSG)

Jesus taught that we should value people over tasks. When we
give as He gave—sharing our time with others, caring for people, and offering comfort where needed—we can experience
life in an unhurried, calm, and peaceful way. It's the perfect way
to understand the "unforced rhythms of grace."

HEAVENLY FATHER, WHEN I MAKE the time to get
away with You, walk with You, and work with You, I experience the divine groove of faith-filled living. When I try to
do things on my own strength, I experience stress and feel
overwhelmed. Like the branch on a vine, I want to abide in
You. Show me how, Lord. I know it's a rhythm; it takes time.
Show me how to practice being in Your presence throughout
my day, no matter what I'm doing. Remind me that You are
always with me, ready to listen, ready to speak. Attune me
to Your voice. You alone have the comfort and peace I need.
In Your presence is fullness of joy. Help me to walk in Your
grace all day long. In Jesus's name, amen.

Have Fun

There is nothing better for a person than that he should eat
and drink and find enjoyment in his toil. This also,
I saw, is from the hand of God.

Ecclesiastes 2:24 (ESV)

When was the last time you had fun? When life gets you down,
lighten up and do something that brings you joy. Nurture your
childlike spirit by picking fresh flowers or going out for ice
cream. Find something that makes you laugh. Do something
you love.

HEAVENLY FATHER, WHEN I'M stressed and looking at
life too seriously, nudge me to seek more joy and laughter.
Please help me find things that just make me giggle. Your
Word says that laughter is good medicine. I know doctors
agree. So remind me to sit, take a deep breath, and then
intentionally look for something that's just plain fun. You
gave us the gift of laughter; help me to use it well. In Jesus's
name, amen.

Napping? Never!

by Elsa Kok Colopy

I jerked awake at the sound of the phone and quickly cleared my throat. "Hello?" I said cheerfully. My friend busted me. "Oh, did I catch you napping?" *Shoot!* I quickly denied it. "Napping? Oh no. Way too busy for that."

After the call ended, I had to laugh at myself. Why the guilt? Why the fear of being caught caring for myself? Napping is a good thing! According to the National Sleep Foundation, studies have found that napping for 20 minutes, what many call a power nap, can reduce daytime sleepiness, boost learning, and improve performance. The National Sleep Foundation suggests an ideal length of time for a nap is 20 minutes, because this amount of time allows your body and mind to rest without going into the deeper stages of sleep. These experts offer some other tips as well:

- Try napping before 2 p.m., so that your sleep doesn't impact your nighttime rest.
- Drink a small amount of caffeine before you rest. It will help you feel less groggy when you wake up, because it takes time for the caffeine to kick in.
- Find a quiet, dark place for your nap.
- To help restore your energy on days you can't take a nap, try spending a little time out in the sunlight.

So next time you feel your eyelids getting heavy as you look longingly toward your bed, give in to it. Stretch out, close your eyes, and breathe deeply. And if a friend happens to call and interrupt, proudly proclaim that you are napping and encourage them to do the same. It's time for us mamas to toss away nap time guilt for good!

My Refuge

If you say, "The LORD is my refuge," and you make the
Most High your dwelling, no harm will overtake you.
Psalm 91:9–10 (NIV)

As a parent, you will most likely face difficulties, fears, and
troubles, and some may be with you a long time. Great news:
God is your refuge! While your problems will not disappear,
when you depend on God to be your stronghold, you will be
able to handle all of them. His goodness and love will always
surround you and will protect and guide you on the path of life.

LORD, WHEN THERE'S A LITERAL storm outside, I seek
shelter. It's the smart thing to do. So when there's a figurative
storm in my life, upsetting everything my heart knows to be
true, remind me to find my shelter in You. I know that no
matter how hard things seem now, forever is longer than
this. Whether it's my kids, my relationships, my job—
whatever is being battered by the winds of worry—shelter
me beneath Your wings. It's in Jesus's name that I pray, amen.

Blessed Interruptions

Commit your way to the LORD; trust in him and he will do this.
Psalm 37:5 (NIV)

Are interruptions and distractions pulling you away from your time with the Lord? Try not to be upset by this. Instead, squeeze in time when you can and make those moments count. When the pressing demands of parenting take you away from your devotional time, avoid the patterns of guilt, tension, or self-blame. Consider that these so-called interruptions may be blessings in disguise and are all part of His plan.

LORD GOD, ALONE TIME with You is precious, especially in the sometimes-harried days of parenting. Please help me to recognize that You are with me all the time. I can talk to You all day long. I can ask for wisdom in every moment. You don't leave me if I have to get up from my chair and tend to something with my child. Help me to be present with You just as I need to be present with my family. Allow me to feel the comfort of just being in the same space together with You while I tend to other tasks. Thank You for never leaving my side and for always listening to my heart. Amen.

The Lighter Side

He will yet fill your mouth with laughter and your lips with shouts of joy.
Job 8:21 (NIV)

If you seize every ounce of laughter and joy that children bring and look for the humor in most situations, you will feel stronger, and your burdens will feel lighter. Play, be silly, grin, guffaw, and laugh. The Lord delights in your joy and the joy you bring to others.

FATHER, I DON'T WANT TO TAKE life so seriously all the time. Hard things happen—sometimes every day—but there is joy in the journey. Remind me to find the humor in situations where I am tempted to feel annoyance. Let laughter be my first response when my child does something just because they're a child. Your Word says that a cheerful heart is good medicine. Help me to lighten up and not take myself, my kids, and our mistakes so seriously. Thank You for the encouragement to laugh. In Jesus's name, amen.

You Are Stronger Than You Think

"Even to your old age and gray hairs
I am he, I am he who will sustain you.
I have made you and I will carry you;
I will sustain you and I will rescue you."

Isaiah 46:4 (NIV)

God has given you a resilient spirit. Humans have endured unspeakable things for generations. The Apostle Paul tells us that suffering produces perseverance; perseverance produces character; and character produces hope. When fear and adversity strike, your spirit will rise to the occasion because God's Spirit lives in you.

DEAR GOD, I DON'T LIKE the process of suffering, but Your Word says that we can rejoice in our suffering because it produces good things in us. So through my adversities, Lord, continue to sustain me. Let me see that the pressure cooker of life is producing in me a tender heart that can better hear Your voice and see Your face. Help me to teach this to my children as well. I want to protect them from suffering, but help me understand that my protection will not produce character in them. Yet I can assure them that I will be by their side, just as You are by mine. I thank You and praise You in Jesus's name, amen.

Releasing a Child into God's Calling— Notes from a Missionary Mom

By Brenda L. Yoder

When my children were young, I'd go into their bedrooms while they were sleeping and pray about my heart's desire for them—that they would love Jesus and follow God's calling in their lives. This seemed like a noble prayer, especially when all four children were under my roof.

As the kids grew older, this prayer faded into the background of our busy family life. When our firstborn and only daughter graduated from high school, that calling took her to a university several states away. Her pursuit of Jesus eventually took her to long-term missionary work in Guatemala and Mexico.

I have often wrestled with God over the faraway places where my daughter and her brothers have settled. All of them live several hours and even several states away. Many days, this is hard. As moms, we naturally want our children close. Then God reminds me that each of my children, though a distance away, is right where they are supposed to be. He *has* answered my prayers that were whispered in their childhood. I am no longer the guide to their life path. God is. Following Jesus's call means His priorities are first in their lives, not my longings for them to be near.

I've learned releasing my children requires letting go of my natural desire to keep them close. It requires trusting God for their life choices and accepting I don't have the same role in their lives that I once did. Instead, God invites me to pray as I did in their childhood, when I confidently trusted God's plan for their futures. It's a posture of faith that lets our children go so they can follow Jesus, no matter where it takes them.

Handover

Jesus replied, "You do not realize now what
I am doing, but later you will understand."
John 13:7 (NIV)

When times are hard and things feel hopelessly out of your control, try to focus on your faith and trust in the One who knows what is best. Instead of putting your energy into trying to force situations to come under your control, use your energy to ask for help in aligning your purpose with His, and place the difficulty firmly into His all-capable hands.

DEAR LORD, IT SEEMS THAT I am always trying to take things out of Your hands. And it never goes well! When will I learn that You are God, and I am not? Today I surrender control to You. You have proven Yourself faithful again and again. You know my yesterdays, todays, and tomorrows. What I can't see, You can see clearly. I don't want to work against Your perfect plan! Nudge me when I start heading in that direction. Help me to trust that You've got it all under control. Thank You for Your patience with me. Amen.

Bless Others

You have many workers: stonecutters, masons and
carpenters, as well as those skilled in every kind of work in
gold and silver, bronze and iron—craftsmen beyond number.
Now begin the work, and the LORD be with you."
2 Chronicles 22:15–16 (NIV)

God gave you unique and special gifts so that your voice and
experience can bless others in meaningful ways. While you might
be tempted to judge yourself harshly and make unflattering
comparisons between yourself and others, remember that
you are wondrously made and have much to offer. Ask God
to show you how to increase the positive difference you are
already making.

CREATOR GOD, THANK YOU for the gifts You have given
me. Sometimes, when I'm just changing diapers, helping
with homework, or providing a listening ear, I can feel like
I'm not doing much good. But the investment I'm making in
my family is so important. Remind me every day that I am
wonderfully made for the tasks You have for me *right now*.
There may be opportunities in the future to do other things,
and that will be great. But I am content with where You have
me today. Help me be a blessing to others right where I am.
When I'm shining Your light, I am doing what You created
me to do. It's in Jesus's name that I pray, amen.

Your Fresh Start

I will give you a new heart and put a new spirit
in you; I will remove from you your heart
of stone and give you a heart of flesh.

Ezekiel 36:26 (NIV)

God offers you a fresh start. As you turn to Him for help and open yourself to His guidance and strength, He will put a renewed spirit in you. Today—at this very moment—you can begin anew!

LORD, SOFTEN MY HEART. Where I have become calloused, pour the oil of Your grace on me. Where I have become rough, sand me down. Thank You that Your mercies are new every morning. Great is Your faithfulness to me! Show me the origins of my stoniness. Get to the root of the problem. If it's pride, root it out. If it's fear, help me to trust You.

Your Spirit brings the fruit of love and joy, peace and patience. Help me to abide in You so that I bear that fruit in abundance. It's in Jesus's name that I pray, amen.

Courage

No one will be able to stand against you all the days of
your life. As I was with Moses, so I will be with you;
I will never leave you nor forsake you.

Joshua 1:5 (NIV)

Wouldn't it be exciting to have an endless supply of courage?
You do! God's wonderful promise to Joshua is also His promise
to you. No matter what life brings, He will never fail or abandon
you or your children. He is your source of courage, a boundless
well of peace and reassurance in this uncertain world.

LORD, I ADMIT TO OFTEN being afraid. I'm afraid I'm
going to parent wrong and my kids are going to be ruined.
I'm afraid of all the stuff that's going on in the world and
what the future holds for my kids. But You hold it all. You are
already in the future. And Your plan for me is perfect. Help
me to let go of my fear and trust You fully, just as Joshua did.
He didn't have it easy, but You were always with him. And
You are always with me. In gratitude I pray, amen.

Teach Us to Pray
by Janet Holm McHenry

As a mom of four very different children, I've watched them over the years as they approached their studies, their friendships, and eventually their college experiences and careers in diverse ways. Their faith walk has varied too, but I've tried to teach each of them how to pray, when to pray, and why:

- Problem-solving. Teaching children to turn to prayer as the best problem-solving strategy is crucial because they can learn to pray for God's help in situations when they need guidance.
- Relational. We can teach children that just as Abraham was called "friend of God" (James 2:23, NKJV), they can have that name too. And just as friends talk with one another, we can talk to God—but anytime we want!
- Therapeutic. When we feel sad and lonely or even angry, we parents can model how we take those feelings to God and let it all out. God heard the laments of Job, David, Jeremiah, and many others in the Bible, so He will hear our emotional prayers too.
- Peace-seeking. Some children get overwhelmed more easily than others. And some simply need more downtime or quiet time on their own. When they discover that prayer time with God brings a sense of calm and peace, they will see prayer as a natural, faith-driven coping mechanism.

Even Jesus's disciples needed to learn to pray. One day one of them said, "Teach us to pray" (Luke 11:1, NIV). So Jesus taught them. As we parents model that prayer is a natural response to our needs, children will follow that example.

Words to Live By

Do not let any unwholesome talk come out of your mouths, but only what is helpful for building others up according to their needs, that it may benefit those who listen.

Ephesians 4:29 (NIV)

Your children are listening. Your words matter. Use them to lift others with encouragement and love. Be sure to tell your loved ones how grateful you are for their presence in your life. Be generous, tender, and forgiving.

DEAR GOD, I KNOW MY WORDS hold power over my children, because I still remember words said to me when I was a child. When I am tempted to speak in anger, Lord, hold my tongue. Help me to speak life. But if I do say something harsh to my kids—or anyone I speak to—help me to quickly ask forgiveness.

Whoever said "words can never hurt me" was so wrong! They do hurt, Lord. And I don't want to be that kind of person. From the overflow of my heart, my mouth will speak, so let my heart be overflowing with Your love. I ask this in Jesus's name, amen.

Prune Your Priorities

He cuts off every branch in me that bears no fruit,
while every branch that does bear fruit he prunes
so that it will be even more fruitful.

John 15:2 (NIV)

Do you feel tired and overwhelmed by all you want to do and
must do in a day as a mom? Try to find a moment to pause
and ask God to help you prioritize. When you turn to Him for
guidance on what is important right now and what can wait for
another day, He will make it all feel more manageable.

HEAVENLY FATHER, I KNOW You are a God of order, not
disorder. There is a time for every purpose under heaven,
but sometimes I try to squeeze it all into one day. That's not
working very well. Help me to take time each day to sit with
You and listen to what it is You want me to do *today*. It's not
all on me, though it can feel like it sometimes. Help me to
advocate for my own mental and physical health so that I
have the capacity to care well for my family. It's in Jesus's
name that I pray, amen.

Now Is the Time

These things I have spoken to you, that my joy
may be in you, and that your joy may be full.
John 15:11 (ESV)

Do you find yourself thinking, *I'll be happy when...*? The next
time you catch yourself postponing happiness, pause for a
moment and experience Jesus pouring joy into your heart.
Because of your faith in the Lord, you do not have to wait for
circumstances to change or time to pass. Because of Him, your
joy can begin right now.

LORD, I KNOW THAT JOY is found in Your presence.
And You are always with me. So if I'm not finding joy in the
here and now, it's because my focus is on the wrong thing.
Turn my eyes back to You. You are always the same; You
will always be loving and gracious and kind toward me. The
truth is, I am not guaranteed tomorrow, so if I don't find
contentment, joy, and peace right now, if I keep waiting for
something more, I am missing out on the joy You want to
give me in this present moment. I'll keep my gaze on Your
face. In Jesus's name, amen.

Rejoice

All who seek the Lord will praise him.
Their hearts will rejoice with everlasting joy.
Psalm 22:26 (NLT)

Every day, God sends blessings and gifts to encourage and
guide us. Many times, our day-to-day responsibilities and tasks
cause us to have our heads down, and we fail to notice His
touch. Today, be aware of His messages of beauty and love.

GRACIOUS FATHER, I HAVE so much to be thankful for.
You are the lifter of my head, so please help me be aware
that I can always find something to rejoice in. Your faithful
presence in my life is one of those things! A beautiful sunset,
a flower blooming in my yard, the quiet of a snowfall, the
sound of my kids' laughter. All these are reasons to praise
You. Remind me to find joy in all that You bring into my life
every day. In Jesus's name, amen.

God's Got This

by Elsa Kok Colopy

My girl was 17 years old and ready to conquer the world as
a junior in high school. Unfortunately, she wasn't making the
best decisions once she ventured out of my sight. She pushed
boundaries on curfew, she fought our rules, she reached for
her independence with a sense of entitlement. We had to put
our foot down and have some hard conversations. Yes, she still
had to be home on time, complete all her homework, honor
us in her tone of voice.

I worried about other things too. Since she was part of the
popular crowd, I worried she might be exposed to drinking
or drugs. Would she have what it took to say no? I petitioned
God. I wrung my hands. I counseled and lectured my daughter
about all the dangers "out there."

Then in the quiet of one worrisome evening, God brought
to my mind the way He captured my heart as a young, way-
ward woman. He had been in the mess. He had been in the
hard. And He had faithfully drawn me to Himself. God reminded me that while my girl may not always be in my sight, she is
always in His. His hand is on her as He constantly works on her
behalf. It might get messy. It might get hard. But He is faithful
to her, and He will never let her go. I held fast to that truth
and let my eyes close in peace.

She is His.

Not Alone

God is our refuge and strength, an ever-present help in trouble.
Psalm 46:1 (NIV)

Being a mother guarantees some unexpected twists and turns in your journey that can be unsettling. Be assured that as you continue to grow in your faith and your desire to live in harmony with God's will, you will realize that there is nothing in this world you have to do alone. He is always with you, guiding you and helping you through life's more challenging—and joyful—times.

FATHER GOD, THANK YOU for being my ever-present help. I don't have to go looking for You; You are always right there. So often I sound like a toddler: "I do it myself!" But I don't need to be that way with You. Your grace strengthens me, and when I am weak, then You are strong. Rid me of my need to be independent! I want to understand what it means to depend on You. In You I live and move and have my being, and I give You praise. Amen.

Rejecting Insecurity

Am I now trying to win the approval of human beings, or of God? Or am I trying to please people? If I were still trying to please people, I would not be a servant of Christ.
Galatians 1:10 (NIV)

No matter how you parent, *someone* will have *something* critical to say. Does this sort of criticism cause you to doubt yourself? Share your concerns with God. Ask Him to help banish your insecurity so you can experience the true peace that comes from knowing that He is in control and has given you all you need to parent well. Relax and rest in Him.

DEAR LORD, I KNOW THAT I am perfectly imperfect. There will always be those who disagree with some of my decisions, who criticize how I parent. But please help me know that You are the only one I need to please. As long as I am seeking Your help and asking advice from trustworthy people, I know that I am on the right path. Thank You for giving me all that I need to be a good mom to my kids. I love them so much! And I love You. In Jesus's name I pray, amen.

Comparison and Competition

Pay careful attention to your own work, for then you will get the satisfaction of a job well done, and you won't need to compare yourself to anyone else.

Galatians 6:4 (NLT)

The word *competition* does not appear in the Bible. Yet how often do we compare ourselves, our children, or our family life with others'? Whether these comparisons create feelings of superiority or envy, turn them over to God. He will help you see that nothing good will come of this sort of competition and comparison. Ask Him to help you celebrate your mothering, your jobs well done, your children, your family, *and* those of others.

FATHER, YOUR GRACE IS SUFFICIENT for me. I believe that with all my heart. But sometimes it's hard to drown out the other voices. Remind me to celebrate the victories no matter how small, to look to You all the time, and then rest in my position as Your child. What anybody else does is not my business. I know You love me unconditionally. Help that fill me with contentment. In Jesus's name, amen.

He Is with You

He is the radiance of the glory of God and the exact
imprint of his nature, and he upholds the universe by the
word of his power. After making purification for sins, he sat
down at the right hand of the Majesty on high.

Hebrews 1:3 (ESV)

Christ is present in every part of your life. Maybe you're too
busy to notice, or maybe you're hoping for or expecting an
earth-shattering sign. Open yourself to His presence. His fin-
gerprints are in the ordinary moments and everyday activities.
During dinner with your family, a quiet moment in devotion,
even grocery shopping—He is with you, blessing your life.

DEAR LORD, THANK YOU FOR ALWAYS being with me.
Even when I can't feel it, I know that You are here because
You promised always to be with me. Your promises are
true. Every tree, every bird, every star in the sky reflects
Your glory. Remind me to take moments throughout my
day to notice all the ways You show me You love me, from
the water, air, and sunlight You created to sustain me to the
amazing creatures and people who grace my life. Thank You
for it all. In Jesus's name, amen.

A Sacred No

by Courtney Ellis

At 11 months pregnant (okay, it was only 8 1/2, but it *felt* like 11!), I was picking up my older son at preschool when his teacher stopped me at the door.

"Would you like to take the class parakeet home?" she asked. I looked down at the sign-up sheet. Every slot was filled except our 9-day spring break. The same window of time as my due date! As I took a breath to say yes, my unborn son kicked me in the ribs and the clipboard clattered to the ground.

"I'll let you know tomorrow," I said, struggling to bend over to pick up what I'd dropped.

At home, I confessed to my husband that we'd be managing a preschooler *and* a parakeet during spring break. He shook his head. "Absolutely not," he said. "You can just say no." I pondered this. *Could* I just say no?

In the Scriptures, Jesus teaches and preaches and heals. He travels all over with His band of disciples. But He also says no an awful lot. And a single refrain is repeated over and over in various forms throughout the Gospels: *I am going to Jerusalem.*

He can say no because He knows what His goal is. He is clear on His purpose. As I pondered the classroom parakeet, I realized I had a singular purpose for spring break: to help our unborn baby into the world safely. It would take all of me to get that done.

The next day I gently told the preschool teacher that I couldn't take the parakeet. Behind me in line another mom piped up, "Can we take it? We love the parakeet!"

Lesson learned: sometimes a proper no makes room for someone else's joyful yes.

Perfectly Imperfect

Though he fall, he shall not be cast headlong,
for the LORD upholds his hand.
Psalm 37:24 (ESV)

How do you handle your mistakes? Do you hold them down deep or accept and release them as part of your growth? God weaves your failures into part of your unique and amazing life. His design for you is built on all that you are—your successes and your disappointments—and they all become part of your beautiful journey.

LOVING FATHER, I KNOW that You love me just as I am, but often this is very hard for me to keep this in mind. I am not perfect, and I make mistakes. Help me to not beat myself up because of my mistakes. When I stumble, pick me up, brush me off, and remind me how much You love me. It's through adversity that I grow. Thank You for being with me through it all. I love You. In Jesus's name, amen.

A Change of Heart

Do not conform to the pattern of this world, but be
transformed by the renewing of your mind. Then you
will be able to test and approve what God's will is—
his good, pleasing and perfect will.

Romans 12:2 (NIV)

Is there something about how you parent that you wish to
change? Maybe you want to make a change in other areas of
your life, such as giving up a bad habit or releasing a grudge.
You can—with Jesus's help! Only Jesus can transform your
heart to be more like His. He can bring blessings to your life.
Ask Him for help.

DEAR LORD, I DON'T HAVE the strength on my own
to change the things in my life that need changing. I'm so
grateful that You are in the redemption business. Take out
what doesn't look like Jesus and transform me to be more
like Him. My impatience, my anger, my desire to please
people, my stubbornness. My pride. Remove it all and fill me
with Your Spirit so that I display the fruit of love, joy, peace,
and patience. Let Your kindness, goodness, faithfulness, and
gentleness shine through me. And build self-control in me.
In Your name, amen.

God's Gift of Forgiveness

Therefore, there is now no condemnation for
those who are in Christ Jesus.

Romans 8:1 (NIV)

Is there something in your past that you struggle to put behind
you? If you are having a hard time forgiving yourself or someone else, talk to God. He longs to transform your life through
the grace of His forgiveness.

HEAVENLY FATHER, SOMETIMES I FEEL hard edges
starting to creep deeper into my heart. My hurt over past
sins threatens to overwhelm me. But I've heard that old
adage: unforgiveness is like drinking poison and hoping the
other person dies. It doesn't work that way. I know that. So
unlock the door of the prison I've put myself in. I don't want
to devalue Jesus's death on the cross for my sins—and the
sins of others. Help me own my own failings and let Jesus
take them away. I ask this in Jesus's name, amen.

Keep Dreaming

Commit to the LORD whatever you do, and
he will establish your plans.
Proverbs 16:3 (NIV)

Sometimes our dreams are a long time coming. Perhaps there
are things on your wish list that seem completely out of reach.
Don't give up. God has given us the ability to look ahead with
hope as well as the drive to keep reaching for our dreams. Is
there a young person in your life with whom you could share
this truth?

LORD, NOTHING IS IMPOSSIBLE with You. I know that
I can make my plans, but ultimately You direct my steps.
Give me discernment to know whether something I want to
accomplish is from You or just from my own desires. What
You have put in my heart, I know You will help me do. You
equip those You call. As I seek to know Your will, I will
better come to know Your heart. And I know that what's on
Your heart, You will accomplish. I want to be part of those
plans. Thank You for using me to glorify Your name. Amen.

Nurturing a Habit of Prayer
through Visual Cues

by Eryn Lynum

"Dear God . . ."

The backseat became quiet as I began praying. My four kids are familiar with this routine. For years, when they were younger, each time we backed out of our driveway, we'd pray aloud together for our day and my husband at work.

I formed this habit before I knew any official language around it. Now habit researchers call this technique a visual cue.

As moms, we understand the power and potential of prayer. Bringing our children to their Creator and Sustainer through consistent and intentional prayer is one of the most significant impacts we can have on their lives and eternities, if not the most significant. But how can we remember to pray among endless laundry, pickups and drop-offs, homework, and activities? Habit experts encourage us to use those things as our visual cues.

With each matched pair of socks, I can pray for that child's feet to carry them to good places.

With each drop-off at an activity, I can pray for protection over their minds, souls, and bodies.

With each difficult school problem, I can pray for their patience and joy in learning.

Rather than trying to remember and grasp my foggy, forgettable intentions, I'm learning to anchor my prayers in things I see or activities I perform each day.

Instead of letting me sit with my good-enough intentions, God is helping me pray consistently—when I start the morning coffee, set the table, and tuck the kids into bed at night.

As I utilize reminders already present in my environment, I can infuse our home with God's presence, peace, and power.

All in God's Time

A thousand years in your sight are like a day that
has just gone by, or like a watch in the night.
Psalm 90:4 (NIV)

Time can seem like an enemy to busy moms. *They grow up too fast! Where did the time go? Hurry, we're going to be late!* It can be helpful to remind ourselves that God controls life's pace. The secret to managing your time is to abide in God, spend time with Him when possible, and place Him firmly in the driver's seat. When you put your relationship with God first, you will find it easier to form a better relationship with time.

DEAR GOD, YOU ARE OUTSIDE of time, but I seem to be chained to it! I know I can't stop the hands of the clock from turning, but I can change my attitude toward it. Help me to slow down and be present in each moment, not looking so far ahead that I fail to see what's important today. I don't want to miss any of my family's important moments because I'm so busy. I know they'll remember time as a family more than any activities. Thank You for the gift of time. Help me to use it well. In Jesus's name I pray, amen.

God of Order

For God is not a God of confusion but of peace.
1 Corinthians 14:33 (ESV)

What mother hasn't wished for more order in her life? The beautiful thing about a strong faith is that it assures you that God is in control, and His Word says that He is a God of order and of peace. Once you believe that deep down in your heart, you will more easily cultivate that order in your life, and your ability to manage the inevitable chaos, clutter, and disorder will improve.

FATHER GOD, NO MATTER how much I might crave order in my life, things so often deteriorate into disorder. I need You! Your peace covering my household will help peace rule in my heart, even when there is a maelstrom around me. Help me to seek You in those moments of chaos so that I have wisdom to know how to bring order to my home. Thank You for being a God of order when so much else is disordered. I am truly grateful. In Jesus's name, amen.

Anxiety Abated

You will be blessed when you come in and
blessed when you go out.

Deuteronomy 28:6 (NIV)

In those times when anxiety begins to tighten its grip on you, sometimes a conscious shift in perspective can help you prevent its escalation. If it is at all possible, pause and remind yourself that God is blessing you right in this moment and in all your moments. Lean on your faith and let His blessing cover you in peace.

FATHER GOD, HELP ME keep my eyes on You. It's so easy to become anxious with all that's going on in my life. But I don't want my worries to rule me. I want Your peace to rule in my life. Remind me of all Your promises for my protection and my provision. Where I might see shortfall, help me see opportunity to watch You work. Help me see what I'm not seeing. You are my strong tower. I can run to You whenever I am afraid. Remind me of that. Thank You for always being there. It's in Jesus's name that I pray, amen.

Positivity Ahead

Finally, brothers and sisters, whatever is true, whatever is
noble, whatever is right, whatever is pure, whatever is lovely,
whatever is admirable—if anything is excellent or
praiseworthy—think about such things.

Philippians 4:8 (NIV)

Okay! Today is the day to decide to face each day with a positive
attitude. Promise yourself and God that you will make an effort
to surround yourself with positive people and to seek out uplifting experiences. You will likely notice that the young people in
your life will pick up on your attitude change and perhaps model
it themselves. If you should find yourself falling into negative
patterns, pause for a moment and ask for God's help to stay on
the positive path.

FATHER, I KNOW IT'S TRUE THAT my mind will dwell
on whatever I fill it with. If I'm surrounded by negativity, my
mind will tend toward negativity. But Your Word encourages
me to let my mind dwell on things that are true and noble
and right. Please guide me to use my time in positive ways.
Help me to be kind and gracious in my speech so that I
reflect Your love to others. In Jesus's name I pray, amen.

Pick Up Sticks

by Peggy Frezon

What if he falls?

What if the equipment fails?

What if he crashes into a tree?

One Saturday morning, I'd planned to pick up the messy branches scattered around my backyard, but instead I found myself collecting the anxious thoughts that cluttered my mind. Earlier that day, my middle-school-age son had cheerfully gone off to an adventure rope course and zip line with a group of friends, chaperoned by a set of their parents. *Keep him safe, God,* I'd prayed. But I continued to worry. *Is he old enough for this?* I bent down to lift a stick and accidentally knocked over a terra-cotta pot by the shed. *Will he be supervised well?* I righted the pot but tripped over my feet and scraped my knee. *Will he attempt something too dangerous?* I overcorrected, stumbled, and nearly fell down a bumpy knoll in the back of my property.

It looked as if I'd had my own adventure course right in my backyard! I thought I'd given my worries over to God, but I kept taking them back, like each little twig I'd lifted off the ground. I hadn't trusted Him to take care of the situation, and my apprehensions prevented me from getting my work done. I took a deep breath. "God, help me to remember that You are watching over Andy while he's away."

Soon I'd gathered a nice pile of sticks. I pulled off my work gloves and went inside. Before long, Andy returned home, in one piece, bubbling with excitement about his adventures. "Thanks, Mom!" he said, giving me a brief hug before disappearing into his room.

"Thanks, God!" I said, knowing that He embraces my son, as well as myself, with an all-consuming love on which I can always rely.

God of Second Chances

Brothers and sisters, I do not consider myself yet to have taken hold of it. But one thing I do: Forgetting what is behind and straining toward what is ahead, I press on toward the goal to win the prize for which God has called me heavenward in Christ Jesus.

Philippians 3:13–14 (NIV)

While it is normal to feel regret about past mistakes or past choices—taken or not taken—regret can cause you to lose out on the joys of here and now. When feelings of regret overtake you, go to God in prayer. He will always be there to guide and help you because He is the God of second chances. He will lead you to leave the past where it belongs and point you in the direction of new beginnings.

DEAR LORD, THANK YOU FOR being the God of second chances. We live in a culture where people are often vilified for their mistakes. I'm so glad You're not like that! I have made many mistakes, but You always give me grace, set my feet back on the right road, and walk beside me. Thank You for Your great love for me. Help me to learn from my mistakes and not beat myself up over them. And help me to give grace to others. For Your name's sake, amen.

God Is Love

And now these three remain: faith, hope and love.
But the greatest of these is love.
1 Corinthians 13:13 (NIV)

"The greatest of these is love," and the greatest thing we can teach our children is love. When love is our motivation and when our actions are guided by selfless love, we can truly experience God's divine and perfect love. Then we can shine a bit of heaven onto those around us.

DEAR GOD, THERE JUST isn't enough that I can say about how amazing Your love is. If I didn't absolutely believe that You love me, I would be lost. And the only reason I can love others is because You first loved me. Please fill me to overflowing with Your love so that it can't help but spill out on others. If ever there is even a hint in my mind that I am unlovable, banish it! I know it is a lie. Thank You for Your faithfulness to me. Amen.

Heavenly Light

For God, who said, "Let light shine out of darkness," made his light shine in our hearts to give us the light of the knowledge of God's glory displayed in the face of Christ.

2 Corinthians 4:6 (NIV)

Two questions to ask yourself today: How are you reflecting God's light by showing kindness, patience, and generosity to others—especially your family? And how can you make that light shine brighter? When God's love shines in your heart, it spreads to everyone you touch.

HEAVENLY FATHER, LET MY HEART be a window to Your love. The more I understand Your love for me, the more I can be a beacon of that love to others. When my own heart isn't right, it's hard to show love to others. Help me immerse myself in Your Word so that I come to truly know You for who You really are. Break down the walls that might have been built in my life that keep me from fully experiencing You. Your love leads me on my way. In Jesus's name I pray, amen.

Divinely Led

And we know that in all things God works for the good of those who love him, who have been called according to his purpose.

Romans 8:28 (NIV)

Sometimes, when we reach out to God, the answer doesn't seem to come. God's intervention is not always obvious. Sometimes He uses indirect circumstances and unlikely people to help us. Sometimes those people are the children in our lives. Listen carefully. Although you may not always be aware of God's hand guiding you, His work will be revealed.

HEAVENLY FATHER, I KNOW that even when I don't feel it, You're moving. Even when I can't see it, You're moving! You have always been faithful, and You always will be faithful because it's who You are. When I am disappointed that You don't do something the way I want it done, remind me that You see the whole story from beginning to end. Similar to the way I can see things my children can't see, Your perspective is greater. Lead me, Lord. I surrender my will to Yours, knowing that You are good. In Jesus's name, amen.

Game Night
by Jeannie Blackmer

One night after a family dinner with our adult sons, daughter-in-law, and a girlfriend, I pulled out a game called Telestrations. This game is based on the old telephone game, where a whispered message is passed from one person to another, but instead of spoken words, this game uses drawings. Everyone starts by writing down a different word in a small dry-erase booklet. Then you pass the booklet with the word you wrote in it to the next person. That person turns the page and draws the word. The booklet gets passed again, and the next person guesses what they think the drawing represents and writes the word for it. The game continues until the booklet returns to the first person.

At the end, each booklet's contents are revealed to the players. It's hysterical. For example, during one game our family played, the original word was "goat cheese," and the final word was "dog taco."

Because I am not gifted with drawing skills, my adult sons argued about who got to sit next to me. They found my indecipherable drawings hilarious. Actually, the truth was, most of us lacked drawing skills. This meant that we all laughed so hard we had tears streaming down our cheeks. The laughter continues. The memory of this game night is brought up frequently when our family gets together, and we laugh all over again.

In a world with so much division, I'm determined to find more silly ways for our family to laugh together. I want to encourage strengthening our bonds as a family, to not take ourselves so seriously, and to all go out into the world with a connecting sense of humor that will spread laughter and joy to others.

Make the Most of Your Time

The life of mortals is like grass, they flourish like a flower
of the field; the wind blows over it and it is gone,
and its place remembers it no more.

Psalm 103:15–16 (NIV)

In the busyness of life, it's easy to forget that time is precious.
As every mother experiences, the time we are given to spend
with our children moves ever so swiftly. Take a moment now to
resolve to always look for ways to spend time wisely and in sync
with God's purpose.

DEAR GOD, LIFE IS SO PRECIOUS. I'm guilty of over-
extending, committing to too many things, and missing
the chance to just *be* with my family. That old adage is so
right: the days are long, but the years are short. Teach me to
number my days. Give me the courage to cut back on what
doesn't need to be done. Remind me to seek You in all my
decisions. And help me find joy in the time we have together
as a family. In Jesus's name, amen.

A Habit of Gratitude

Bless the LORD, O my soul, and forget not all his benefits.
Psalm 103:2 (ESV)

Developing a habit of gratitude will improve your life and the lives of those around you. Dr. Norman Vincent Peale said, "A basic law: the more you practice the art of thankfulness, the more you have to be thankful for. This, of course, is a fact. Thankfulness does tend to reproduce in kind." When you wake up each morning, give thanks for the day ahead. Each night, before you sleep, spend a few minutes counting all your blessings and thanking God for each of them.

DEAR LORD, I DO HAVE so much to be thankful for. If I focus only on my circumstances, I can have the tendency to grumble. So please expand my vision, Lord. For each sunrise, the laughter of my child, my friends, a roof over my head, let me give You praise. And help me teach my children to be grateful as well. Like me, they can want so much and forget what they already have. Never let me lose sight of my blessings, the chief of which is Your presence in my life. It's in Jesus's name that I pray, amen.

Plant Yourself in God's Word

Yes, my soul, find rest in God; my hope comes from him.
Psalm 62:5 (NIV)

When you feel that the world is chaotic and spinning out of control, center your heart on God and His Word. You may find it helpful to have a few verses committed to memory to focus on in these times. Then it will take only a moment to pause, breathe deeply, and reflect on His Word. Root yourself in passages that focus on His profound peace.

DEAR LORD, THANK YOU for the gift of Your Word and for all the people who have made it accessible to us. I'm so grateful that I can find encouragement in Your love letter to me all the time. As I immerse myself in the Bible, I get to know You better, which fills me with peace. Help me stay grounded in Your Word so that the winds of doubt and distress don't carry me away. It's in Your name that I pray, amen.

Answered Prayers

Ask and it will be given to you; seek and you will find;
knock and the door will be opened to you.

Matthew 7:7 (NIV)

Even if the word *journaling* sends a shiver down your spine, you
might want to try this experiment. For a short period of time,
jot down all your prayers—all of them, including the important
ones and the mundane ones, such as *Help me find a good
parking spot.* No need for a fancy book; just a few pieces of
paper that you can carry and keep close by will do. Then record
the answers you receive. You will be astounded by the results!

FATHER GOD, YOU KNOW what I need. No matter what
I think I *want*, You always know what I *need*. Help me to
have open eyes, an open heart, and open hands to what You
want to provide for me. Nothing is too trivial to talk to You
about, because I know You love me and just want to be with
me. Please help me see where You're working in my life, and
show me how I can grow my relationship with you. In Jesus's
name, amen.

Exchanging Burdens for Blessings

By Brenda L. Yoder

I once heard that a mother is never happier than her saddest child. I've learned this truth as an empty-nest mom. It's often heart-wrenching when your grown children are brokenhearted or experiencing loss. When kids are younger or at home under your roof, you are more involved in mending their broken hearts. But the stance of carrying their burdens is different when they are adults. You have less control over the outcomes, which can make the burden heavier.

There was a season when my adult children experienced pain and loss simultaneously. The load was heavy and hard because I couldn't predict how the situation would turn out or promise a silver lining. I kept telling my kids that God promised hope and a future for them, based on Jeremiah 29:11.

I was challenged to put authentic faith behind God's promise. God could turn my children's burdens into blessings, right? I often came to God in tears as I poured out grief only a mother understands. When I didn't know how to pray, Jesus reminded me He was interceding for me. He invited me to lay my burdens at the cross, the place of sorrow. It was a feeling Jesus understood more than I could ever imagine.

The transformation began when, instead of lingering in lament, I prayerfully exchanged my spirit of heaviness for the future blessings God has planned for my children. This exchange became a rhythm in my prayer life. Soon, peace and lightness filled my mind and heart. Jesus carried the burden— the load was no longer mine. Encouraging words to my kids came more confidently and genuinely. I began praising God for the blessings He was already preparing.

Follow the Good Shepherd

When he has brought out all his own, he goes before
them, and the sheep follow him, for they know his voice.

John 10:4 (ESV)

It is not easy, but it *is* possible to hear and know God's voice. It
takes intention and a little practice to listen deeply. Then, when
the Shepherd guides you, follow Him.

FATHER, HELP ME BE SO accustomed to Your voice that I
can spot a counterfeit a mile away. There are a lot of voices
trying to vie for my attention. I want to hear Yours. You will
never lead me astray, and Your will is always for my good.
Guide me to listen more carefully. In the name of Jesus I
pray, amen.

Embrace the New

Behold, I am doing a new thing; now it springs forth,
do you not perceive it? I will make a way in the
wilderness and rivers in the desert.

Isaiah 43:19 (ESV)

How do you encourage yourself and the ones you are mothering
to try something new? Do you set an example by trying new
foods and new hobbies, taking an unfamiliar route, or reading a
different book genre? By embracing the new and being adventurous, you never know what new favorite thing God will invite
into your life.

DEAR GOD, YOU ARE INFINITELY creative, but I can
get stuck in a rut. Routines are good, I know, but flexibility,
spontaneity, creativity—they keep me from tunnel vision.
Tune my heart to see You and how You work in new ways
as well. Let my life reflect Your creativity as I try new things
and encourage my children to do the same. It's in Jesus's
name I pray, amen.

Do Away with Doubt

But when you ask, you must believe and not doubt,
because the one who doubts is like a wave
of the sea, blown and tossed by the wind.
James 1:6 (NIV)

When doubt creeps in, we feel unsettled and unbalanced.
During those times when you feel your faith becoming un-
steady and you take on the weight of all your problems yourself, the situation only becomes worse. Take a moment to gently steer your mind and spirit back to God. Know with certainty
that He will carry you through challenging circumstances calmly
and safely.

FATHER GOD, AS THE DESPERATE father in the Bible
cried out to You, "I do believe; help me overcome my unbelief!" (Mark 9:24, NIV), I also cry out to You. I have seen
Your faithfulness so many times. Help me not to doubt in
the darkness what I believed in the light. David trusted You
with his whole heart, even when he cried out in despair. I
know that You are good, so when times look bleak, when I
can't see Your hand, I will cling to that truth. In the powerful
name of Jesus I pray, amen.

An Open Door

See, I have placed before you an open door
that no one can shut.
Revelation 3:8 (NIV)

Parenting can be fraught with obstacles, and it is not unusual to feel trapped by circumstances. It is important to remember that God always has an open door for you—a way, a choice, an entrance to a better way of thinking or feeling about what you are experiencing. The next time you are feeling stuck in some way, pause to ask God to show you the open door.

DEAR GOD OF REDEMPTION, You always make a way where there seems to be no way. You brought the Israelites out of Egypt and parted the sea for them. You raised Lazarus from the dead when his family and friends thought he was gone forever. You fed five thousand people from five small loaves and two fish. You *always* make a way. Bring peace to my heart with the knowledge that You see me and You are working for my good. Tune my heart to hear Your voice. In Jesus's name I pray, amen.

More Than One Way to Be a Mom
by Peggy Frezon

My daughter Kate placed the baby on a soft blanket on the floor. "It's tummy time," Kate said. The baby kicked her legs and cooed.

"Tummy time? We never had tummy time when you were little." My brow furrowed a bit.

"Well, things are different now," Kate answered.

Later, at nap time, Kate tucked my granddaughter in a cozy sleeper and laid her on her back in the crib.

"When you were little, babies were supposed to sleep on their sides," I said.

"Well, things are different now," Kate said again, putting her arm around me as we left the nursery.

Sometimes I felt like Kate and I were totally different moms. I used to keep charts and schedules. She was much more relaxed. I rocked my babies to sleep. She let them fuss themselves to sleep. I boiled the pacifier when it hit the floor. She didn't worry about that. How could our philosophies be so different?

That evening, I peeked into the nursery. The room was lit only by a lamp that illuminated Kate in the rocking chair, the children in their cozy footie pajamas snuggled on her lap. She turned the page of a book. "'In the beginning, God made everything,'" Kate read. "'He made the trees and the water and the animals, and He made us. And everything was perfect.'"

I felt as if I'd received a warm hug. "I remember snuggling with you and reading you Bible stories when you were little," I whispered.

Kate smiled. "I guess some things aren't so different now."

My daughter and I may not always be on the same page, and child-rearing practices may always change. But making a priority of putting God first in parenting, as well as in life, is timeless.

True Value

*And the world is passing away along with its desires,
but whoever does the will of God abides forever.*
1 John 2:17 (ESV)

How do you determine your worth? Do your confidence and happiness shift depending on how much you or your children accomplish, your career trajectory, or how you compare yourself to others? If you change your focus from these worldly concerns to align yourself with God's will, you'll discover a new peace. Psalm 119 offers good advice: "Turn my eyes away from worthless things; preserve my life according to your word" (verse 37, NIV).

DEAR FATHER, I KNOW I am Your child. Nothing can take that away from me, and there's nothing I can do to earn more of Your love. You already love me fully! When I begin comparing myself to others, stop me in my tracks. When I think I need to compete for attention, remind me that Your eyes are always on me, and You know the number of hairs on my head. I am worthy because You call me worthy. What freedom this brings! Thank You for Your steadfast love. In Jesus's name, amen.

Seasons of Change

He has made everything beautiful in its time. Also, he has put eternity into man's heart, yet so that he cannot find out what God has done from the beginning to the end.
Ecclesiastes 3:11 (ESV)

The cycles in life, the seasons of change, are completely natural and part of God's order. But it doesn't always seem so in times of turmoil, pain, and uncertainty. When you need reassurance and guidance, turn to the Source of all wisdom in prayer. He will help sustain you through it all.

FATHER GOD, JUST AS I ENJOY the changing seasons of the year, help me to appreciate the changing seasons in my life. I know that the good and natural thing is for children to grow up and create lives of their own. Sometimes this is a painful thought for me; it's hard to let go. Help me respect and cherish the seasons of their lives and to trust You with all things. Thank You for walking with me through it all. I praise You in Jesus's name, amen.

Your Prayers

Behold, I stand at the door and knock. If anyone
hears my voice and opens the door, I will come
in to him and eat with him, and he with me.

Revelation 3:20 (ESV)

Prayer is your personal conversation with God. Your words,
your feelings, your conversations with Him are based on the
unique and blessed relationship that continues to grow the
more you pray. "Blessed be God, because he has not re-
jected my prayer or removed his steadfast love from me!"
(Psalm 66:20, ESV).

LORD GOD, IT NEVER CEASES to amaze me that You
want to spend time with me. But You have called me Your
own. I am Your precious child. And unlike me, who sometimes needs a break from my kids, You never grow tired of
being with me! Thank You for listening to my every word,
for knowing my every thought, for answering my every
prayer in Your will and for Your glory. The invitation is
always open to talk with You. It's an amazing privilege, and
I am grateful. In Jesus who makes it all possible, amen.

The Wisdom of Not Knowing

*Let the wise hear and increase in learning, and the
one who understands obtain guidance.*
Proverbs 1:5 (ESV)

It is okay to not know everything, to not know what you want
or how to make things better. When you say, "I don't know,"
it opens the door to finding out, to thinking and discovering.
Through prayer, ask for God's help and then wait patiently for
His answer.

HEAVENLY FATHER, I DON'T HAVE all the answers, but
I know that You do. Even when I lose something, You know
right where it is. Sometimes You show me, and sometimes
You don't. I trust Your wisdom. You have also given me a
sound mind, and sometimes You want me to wrestle with
an issue. But You are always there to give me the wisdom I
need. Help me admit when I don't know the answers. Help
me model to my children that relying on You is the right
path, and that "I don't know" is sometimes the right answer.
In Jesus's name, amen.

A Nature Trail to the Gospel Message

by Eryn Lynum

I watched as my three-month-old daughter lay on a blanket at the park. Her three older brothers played on the playground while she and I sat beneath the shade of a tree. Her eyes were alert and filled with wonder as she watched swaying leaves above. Recently, she'd discovered the beginnings of mobility by scooting herself on her back a tiny distance at a time. This morning, she practiced her newfound freedom by inching her way to the edge of the blanket until her little toes brushed against fresh grass. I watched surprise flush her face at the new sensation. She pushed her feet back and forth, exploring the natural world through the soles of her feet long before she would ever walk.

My daughter is five now, and her favorite way to spend a morning is running barefoot through the grass. My prayer for her is that these experiences in nature will prepare the soil of her heart for the gospel. She has heard the good news of Jesus's death and resurrection since we brought her home, and that message has been coupled with experiences in God's creation.

When my children were too young to understand Christ's sacrifice and the gift of grace through faith, they could still sense the power and presence of a Creator in the breeze off the ocean or in a star-studded night sky. While nature cannot communicate the intricacies of salvation, I know time outdoors has prepared their minds and hearts to embrace an incredible God who creates good things and is making all things new.

As it says in Romans 1:20 (NIV), "Since the creation of the world God's invisible qualities—his eternal power and divine nature—have been clearly seen, being understood from what has been made, so that people are without excuse."

Behold

God saw all that He had made, and behold, it was very good.
Genesis 1:31 (NASB)

Today. At this very moment. Take a good look at the world around you and all the beauty in nature, your family, your friends, and your life. You are surrounded by miracles! Take a moment to engage all your senses to experience God's miraculous gifts.

LORD, YOU HAVE CREATED so much beauty! In all times, remind me of Your good gifts. When I look at my children, I realize what a miracle they are. When I look out the window at night, the stars are singing of Your majesty. When I take a walk or just step outside for a few moments, the trees sway their branches in praise of Your glory. Thank You for allowing me to experience all this splendor. Amen.

Progress, Not Perfection

Surely there is not a righteous man on earth
who does good and never sins.

Ecclesiastes 7:20 (ESV)

Don't be so hard on yourself. Seek excellence, not perfection. When you reflect on your goals and where you are in your life, focus on signs of progress. Celebrate small wins and big strides and help your children learn how to do this as well. You all deserve to feel good about yourselves!

HEAVENLY FATHER, PERFECTIONISM is a ball and chain. Sometimes it prevents me from accomplishing what I need to, because I don't want to do it if I can't do it perfectly. I know this is utterly ridiculous. Help me to throw off the chains of perfectionism and live in freedom to make mistakes, to learn from them, and to take the next step forward. Help me to celebrate even the smallest of victories. And help me not to listen to any voices that would tell me I'm not good enough. Thank You for Your love and grace. In Jesus's name, amen.

Angels Watching Over

For he will order his angels to protect you wherever you go.
Psalm 91:11 (NLT)

God is watching over you, and His amazing kindness surrounds
and guides you and your family. Assure your children that
they can go through life with a contented spirit, knowing God
watches over them—no matter what comes their way.

LOVING FATHER, YOU HAVE PROMISED to never leave
me nor forsake me, and I know You always keep Your promises. Even if I *feel* alone, I know that I am not. Remind me
to trust in Your promises. All Your ways are good, and I can
trust that You are working all things out for my good. Whenever I am afraid, help me to turn to You. When my children
run to me when they're scared, I don't turn them away. And
I know You won't turn me away either. Thank You for Your
steadfast love. In Jesus's name, amen.

Gratitude in Your Heart

Let the peace of Christ rule in your hearts, since as members
of one body you were called to peace. And be thankful.
Let the message of Christ dwell among you richly as you
teach and admonish one another with all wisdom through
psalms, hymns, and songs from the Spirit, singing
to God with gratitude in your hearts.

Colossians 3:15–16 (NIV)

Starting today, make it a practice to start each day with gratitude
in your heart. Gratitude in and of itself is a form of peace. When
you recognize your blessings, both commonplace and extraordinary, you open your heart to feel God's presence.

DEAR GOD, I AM GRATEFUL FOR ALL that You have
given me, and for all that You are in my life. When I focus
on what I have instead of what I don't have, I have so much
more peace. The message of the world is that we should not
be content with what we have, but that we should want more
and more. This puts pressure on us to keep working at being
content instead of just resting in You. I'd rather rest. Thank
You for Your peace. In Jesus's name, amen.

Imaginative Prayer
by Jeannie Blackmer

When I became a mom to three teenage boys who pushed the thrill-seeking envelope, strove for independence, and made choices with difficult consequences, especially one son who was abusing alcohol, I found it hard to know what or how to pray.

Out of desperation, I searched the New Testament for parents who sought out Jesus on behalf of their children. I found several, including a ruler, two mothers, and a father in the book of Matthew. I've always looked at these dialogues with Jesus as interactions showing the power He has and the miracles He performed when He walked the Earth. But after more closely reading them, my perspective shifted. I began to see these conversations between parents and Jesus as prayers.

Their exchanges expressed my own feelings. Like me, these parents were begging Jesus for help in some hard situations. These dialogues—authentic and emotional—became my prayers.

Using my imagination, I started picturing myself in their place, adapting their requests to my desires for my children, asking Jesus to intervene in my own children's lives. For example, I saw myself as the mom who faithfully pursued healing for her daughter from a demon in Matthew 15:22. I adapted her words for my prayer: "Lord, heal my son from alcohol addiction." Alcohol was the "demon" in my son's life. I inserted my needs and requests into these verses and situations and created powerful and powerfully personal prayers. It's a technique I still practice.

God has gifted us with an imagination. So, as I imagined myself with Jesus, I experienced His healing words, comfort, and listening heart. Using this practice of imaginative prayer, I talk with Jesus anytime, anywhere about anything—even when I'm at a loss for words.

Grow in Christ

But grow in the grace and knowledge of our Lord and Savior
Jesus Christ. To him be glory both now and forever! Amen.

2 Peter 3:18 (NIV)

As you know, spiritual growth is a lifelong process. Even as you
guide your children in their spiritual growth, yours multiplies.
The closer you grow to God, the more you realize how much
more there truly is! God's bounteous gifts are infinite.

HEAVENLY FATHER, MY HELP comes from You all day,
every day. There is so much I don't know! I want to grow in
my knowledge and in grace. Your Word says that knowledge
without love is useless. I can know everything there is to
know, but if I don't have love, it's just noise. Please help me
to nurture my relationship with You as I help my children
learn more about Your love and grace. Thank You for letting
us have these glimpses of Your glory as we wait to see You
face-to-face. In Jesus's name I pray, amen.

When to Say No

For God gave us a spirit not of fear but of power
and love and self-control.

2 Timothy 1:7 (ESV)

As a mom, you've certainly heard that knowing when to say no or ask for help is important. Easier said than done, right? It can't happen overnight, but you *can* build your discernment. Learning to recognize when it's time to say no, downsize your responsibilities, or ask for help is the first step toward easing your burden. The good news is that when you empty your cup of what you cannot hold, you make room for new blessings.

GREAT AND AWESOME GOD, give me the courage to say no and to ask for help. You gave me a sound mind to be able to discern when I'm taking on too much or caring too much about what others think. You made me for community, so help me to lean on my community when I need tangible help. Remind me that saying no doesn't make me a bad person and that, when it's appropriate, it is an indication of my growing wisdom. I ask this in Jesus's name, amen.

Build Sandcastles

I know that there is nothing better for people than
to be happy and to do good while they live.
Ecclesiastes 3:12 (NIV)

Anne Frank once said, "I don't think building sandcastles in the air is such a terrible thing to do, as long as you don't take it too seriously." Building sandcastles is sometimes used as a metaphor for wasting time. But if you build a sandcastle with a child, you demonstrate how to value something, have fun, and savor the moment. You also help build their understanding that so much of what is around us is temporary.

HEAVENLY FATHER, REMIND ME that it is never a waste to be playful and enjoy the day. You gave us all things to enjoy and to bring You glory. Thank You for the gift of laughter, for joy, for things that make us happy. It's good to enjoy the life You gave us and to have unfiltered moments of happiness. Remind me of this throughout my day. Help me take time to just laugh at something silly with my kids. I pray in the name of Jesus, amen.

Time to Rest

Come to Me, all you who labor and are heavy laden,
and I will give you rest.
Matthew 11:28 (NKJV)

While there is certainly joy in being a mom, the demands of parenthood are immense. Physical and mental exhaustion can take their toll. Before frustration and irritability take hold, try to find ways to nurture yourself and recharge. Carve out a few quiet moments here and there, and lean into your faith, realizing that by forming a closer relationship with God, you can give your best self to your children.

LORD, I NEED YOU. EVERY HOUR I need You. I can't do anything on my own strength. Turn my eyes away from the things the world tells me I have to do and turn them toward You. You give me rest. Your burden is light. Oh, how I long for a lighter load. Remind me that I don't have to be perfect. That's impossible anyway. I just need to be with You. When Your peace covers my life, I can be a better mom, a better friend, a better employee. You make me better. Help me never to forget this. In Your holy name I pray, amen.

The Mentoring Spirit of Motherhood
by Brenda L. Yoder

When I married into a farm family, my mother-in-law became a mentor to me. Farm life presented me with a different lifestyle than I was accustomed to. Lois taught me the rhythms and responsibilities of a young farmwife and mom. When she unexpectedly died, I grieved for the loss of her intricate presence in my life and in the lives of my young children. I often felt lost in my grief and sadness. She was the person I went to for wisdom, encouragement, and the practical skills of motherhood. Outside of my mother, I wondered who would help me and serve as a supportive presence in my life.

A few months after Lois's death, a note came in the mail from an older woman in our congregation. Her words encouraged me in my grief and were just what I needed. The letter let me know other women were around me who had a caring spirit like Lois's. As time passed and the children grew older, another woman took me under her wing, supporting me in ways I knew Lois would have.

These older women gently filled the hole left by a mom and grandma who was greatly missed. This experience gave me eyes of empathy to see young moms in my life who have needed extra support under challenging experiences or in times of loss. Having a nurturing mentor when I felt most alone or discouraged has prompted me to reach out to other moms as I've grown older. I've tried to offer an encouraging word or a helpful task, or be a more long-term presence in the lives of younger women who need the compassionate spirit of a mother-like figure. I hope to be that protective, caring, mentor-mom who emulates what others have been to me.

When God Seems Silent

To You, O LORD, I call; my rock, do not be deaf to me.
For if You are silent to me, I will become like
those who go down to the pit.

Psalm 28:1 (NASB)

Sometimes in your prayer life it might seem as if God is quiet—that maybe He is not present or hearing you. If this happens to you, continue praying. You may find it helpful to keep track of your prayers and how you feel. Often you'll discover that what appears to be a desert period in your prayer life has brought about the most beautiful blossoms.

FATHER GOD, THANK YOU for the beauty and comfort of David's psalms. Please remind me that You hear me and that I am not alone. Give me patience, Lord, to know that You don't work on my timeline but that You are always working. Even when I can't see it, You are working all things together for my good and Your glory. Amen.

An Extra Hour

Making the best use of the time, because the days are evil.
Ephesians 5:16 (ESV)

If you feel that there is never enough time, ask yourself, *If I'd had one extra hour today, what would I have spent it doing?* Then, tomorrow, try making that endeavor the first thing you do. This experiment in shifting priorities may help you manage your time better and help you have more control over how you spend your time.

HEAVENLY FATHER, I KNOW there are only 24 hours in a day. I know how many waking hours I have. Yet somehow I always wish I had more. But You had a reason for setting the Earth's orbit the way You did. So I know I need to make some changes. Prioritizing my time with You is first on the list. When this happens, my soul will be so much more at peace. When I'm harried and hurried, I don't reflect You. Keep me mindful of how I spend my time. I ask in Jesus's name, amen.

Are You Joyful?

Nehemiah said, "Go and enjoy choice food and sweet drinks,
and send some to those who have nothing prepared.
This day is holy to our Lord. Do not grieve,
for the joy of the LORD is your strength."
Nehemiah 8:10 (NIV)

Children often observe their parents to gauge the mood of the
household and take the cues. Are you joyful, no matter your
circumstances? Perhaps Dr. Norman Vincent Peale's words
will help. He said, "Think excitement, talk excitement, act out
excitement, and you are bound to become an excited person.
Life will take on a newness, deeper interest, and greater mean-
ing. You can think, talk, and act yourself into dullness or into
monotony or into unhappiness. By the same process you can
build up inspiration, excitement, and surging depth of joy."
What are you talking yourself into?

LORD GOD, GUIDE MY THOUGHTS away from my problems and onto my blessings. Focus my actions on bringing
others joy. If I look for joy, if I find my strength in the joy of
the Lord, I know that my attitude and my heart will change.
I don't want to be known as someone living under a dark
cloud. I want the bright light of Jesus to show through my
words and my actions. In Your presence is fullness of joy. In
Jesus's name I pray, amen.

The Hardest Part

Wait for the LORD; be strong and take
heart and wait for the LORD.
Psalm 27:14 (NIV)

Sometimes God calls us to wait and not act. Poll a group of people in your life, and chances are not one of them will say they're *good* at waiting. Still, we're called on to do so—more often than we like. When these times occur, try to remind yourself of your commitment to trust God, to surrender your will to His, and to exchange your timing for His. Know that God holds every moment in His hands.

HEAVENLY FATHER, YOU KNOW THAT I'm not good at waiting! But You also know that I'm aware of the risks of taking things into my own hands. You are faithful, and You are good. If I want my kids to learn how to wait for the things they want, I need to model that for them. Thank You for Your patience with me. Let the fruit of patience spring forth as I abide in You, and let the Holy Spirit live through me. Amen.

Exercise Your Prayer Life

by Janet Holm McHenry

Some say families that play together, stay together. Others also say families that *pray* together, stay together. What if we put those two together—play and prayer—to create strong memories for children as well as a compassionate mindset? Let's go for a prayer-walk!

Prayer-walking is praying for what and whom we see as we walk through our communities. As we walk, my children and I say short, specific prayers for what and whom we observe, such as families in their homes, squirrels in the trees, people driving by, and more. The prayers can be simple—something children can easily understand: "God, bless this family and give them peace." "Heavenly Father, keep that man and his dog safe and help them see the joy in Your beautiful creation." It's a natural physical and spiritual activity for children because of their innate curiosity and awareness of their surroundings.

Here are some simple suggestions for prayer-walking with your kids:

- Decide on a specific day and time for prayer-walking and try to stick to your plan.
- Dress in appropriate clothing and footwear for the weather.
- Teach your children to be aware of traffic. Always face oncoming traffic and look carefully before crossing streets.
- Carry personal identification and your cell phone with you, and choose safe places to walk.
- Start out slowly, then pick up your pace. Prayer-walking can provide good exercise, but don't let it turn into a race.
- Teach your child to look for prayer needs. For example, if you see an upset mom, say to them, "Let's pray God helps that mom."
- Most important, just enjoy the time together!

God Doesn't Make Mistakes

This God—his way is perfect; the word of the LORD proves
true; he is a shield for all those who take refuge in him.

Psalm 18:30 (ESV)

We know we learn much from our own mistakes. We can also
learn and grow closer to God when we experience other people's mistakes. When a small mistake or something unexpected
happens, such as a wrong number, a wrong turn, or a missed
meeting, try this: Use it as an opportunity to trust in God's way
and say a quick prayer of thanksgiving. Often mistakes turn out
to be detours that bring blessings.

DEAR LORD, THANK YOU FOR PROVIDING me with
such a rich supply of teachable moments, because I make
a lot of mistakes! But Your ways are perfect and just. It's a
valuable lesson I want my children to learn: We make mistakes, we learn from them, and we move on better than we
were before. I especially want to demonstrate this perspective with my kids. They're going to mess up, so help my
reaction to be one of grace and helping them learn how to
do better the next time. It's what You do for me. And I'm so
grateful. With praise and thanksgiving I pray, amen.

Patience

Be joyful in hope, patient in affliction, faithful in prayer.
Romans 12:12 (NIV)

When you are in a state of distress or misery, having patience can seem nearly impossible. Periods of waiting can be especially hard on one's faith. In stressful times, when nothing seems to be going right, it's important to remind yourself that God is in control. Hold on; keep your hope and faith alive. He will give you the desires of your heart in His time.

DEAR LOVING FATHER, IF I LOSE HOPE, I lose everything. When I put my trust fully in You, I can wait for anything. I know that without faith, it is impossible to please You. I know that You don't mind me asking for things and that You don't want me just striking out on my own to get what I want. Please help me to grow in patience as I learn more and more about Your character. You are good and You will always provide what I need. In Jesus's name I pray, amen.

Life's Curves

And though the Lord give you the bread of adversity and the water of affliction, yet your Teacher will not hide himself anymore, but your eyes shall see your Teacher. And your ears shall hear a word behind you, saying, "This is the way, walk in it," when you turn to the right or when you turn to the left.
Isaiah 30:20–21 (ESV)

Have you ever reflected on your life journey up to this moment and felt like you've backtracked? Perhaps in hindsight an unexpected detour felt like wasted time, or a distraction or missed opportunity led you to believe you had lost your way. Life's twists and turns sometimes don't make sense to us, but the good news is that when you follow God, you can trust that you are on the right road.

HEAVENLY FATHER, I HAVE FAITH THAT I am always on a straight path when I stay close to You. You will not let my foot slip. The psalmist declared that even if I walk through the dark valley, You are always with me. You bring me comfort. When my life takes a circuitous route, You stay by my side, always urging me to walk in the light of Your Word. Give me ears to hear Your voice, even in the darkness. I trust You to never lead me astray. In Jesus's name I pray, amen.

Overflowing Blessings

The one who blesses others is abundantly blessed;
those who help others are helped.

Proverbs 11:25 (MSG)

One of the many beautiful concepts of faith is the ever-multiplying cycle of blessings. You can nurture your connection with God by pausing for a moment to say a prayer that blesses someone. Imagine them surrounded by God's holy light, basking in His kindness, mercy, and goodness. In being a blessing to others, you are living out part of God's purpose for you. In turn, you will be abundantly blessed.

FATHER GOD, YOU HAVE BLESSED me so that I may be a blessing to others. The gifts You have given me aren't meant to be hoarded. Even my prayers are not meant to be for me alone. Show me every day how I can share what I have with others. My time, my treasure, my talents—they're all meant to be used to bless others. And the thing of it is, in Your economy, I'll be the one enriched the most. Thank You. In Jesus's name, amen.

Prayer Walks

by Julie Lavender

One of the activities I've enjoyed about living in an empty nest is the opportunity to take long walks in the morning. I admit, when the house bubbled over with toddlers and turmoil, middle schoolers and mayhem, and adolescents and activity, I didn't focus on my own health. There simply wasn't time.

In hindsight, perhaps I should have found time for exercise and better self-care, but I'm trying to make up for it now. At first, I felt guilty when I started daily jaunts, because even with an empty house, I still had much to do. My to-do list loomed large: prayer time, writing deadlines, errands for my ailing mom, church responsibilities, laundry, housekeeping, and cooking.

Ever the multitasker, I began to wonder if I could combine prayer with my morning walks, and I gave it a try. I quickly found that I could focus more and concentrate better on my time with the Lord when I was walking. When I was sitting in my previous prayer spot, the front porch swing, I was much more easily distracted, and my prayers, though heartfelt, could be disjointed.

Walking serves a two-fold purpose in my conversations with God. Most noticeably, His beautiful creations usher me into His presence. Secondly, away from my house, I don't feel the pull of responsibilities waiting for me inside.

I also find that praying aloud keeps me focused. Walking and talking with God truly gives me the feeling I'm actually walking and talking with God—as if He's right by my side.

My nest may be empty, but my heart is not. I spend most of my prayer time talking with God about my four children, two sons-in-love, and one grandson. What could be better?

God Will Rescue You

He reached down from on high and took hold
of me; he drew me out of deep waters.

2 Samuel 22:17 (NIV)

Have you ever found yourself in deep waters—in over your
head and drowning in difficulties? Most of us have. These
situations can pull us into a place of darkness and emotional
turmoil. Reach out to God in prayer and ask for His hand. Offer
Him your worries and fears. Let Him rescue you.

LORD GOD, AS A DROWNING PERSON sometimes fights
their rescuer because of fear, I know I can fight against You
when I am afraid. Help me understand that You are here for
me. When I'm overwhelmed, awash in trials and difficulties,
please speak softly to me and calm my fears. Your steadfast
love endures forever. You have never left me when times
have been hard. I know You won't leave me now. Just as I
taught my children when they were learning to float in the
water, I want to relax and trust You to hold me and never let
me go. In Jesus's name I pray, amen.

Love First

Be devoted to one another in love. Honor
one another above yourselves.
Romans 12:10 (NIV)

Mothers are often called upon to put their family's needs and well-being above their own. We know the element of sacrifice that accompanies deep, abiding love. We demonstrate unselfishness for our children and help them expand and mature their perception of love. As we free our hearts from jealousy, pettiness, and resentment, our love grows, and our spirits are filled. We are instruments of His work.

DEAR LORD, I LOVE BECAUSE You first loved me. The only reason I can love at all is because of You. When I hold a grudge, or grumble about someone else, I am not showing love, nor am I modeling it for my children. Forgive me, Lord. Help me to see everyone through Your eyes. They are Your image bearers and deserve dignity and love. Help me to shine the light of Your love no matter whom I'm with. It's all because of Jesus. Amen.

Practice Stillness

He says, "Be still, and know that I am God; I will be
exalted among the nations, I will be exalted in the earth."
Psalm 46:10 (NIV)

Great expanses of time for stillness and quiet elude most of us.
Still, we can look for the moments and small bits of time when
we can be still and silent and listen to God's gentle whisper. As
we open our hearts to His presence, our stillness also speaks to
Him. As with good friends enjoying the moment, words aren't
necessary.

LORD, I SOMETIMES FORGET the importance of being
still. Quiet really does restore my soul. But it also connects
me to You. I can't hear You when there's so much noise
around me. You are not in the earthquake or the fire or the
storm. You are in the still, small voice. Much of the noise
in my life is of my own making. Quiet me, Lord. Bring rest
to my heart. Remind me that I don't have to do it all; I just
need to... *be.* It's in Your name that I pray, amen.

Let the Spirit Lead

"For the Holy Spirit will teach you at that
time what you should say."
Luke 12:12 (NIV)

Are you afraid to speak publicly or do you find yourself
sometimes unable to find the words to speak—maybe out of
shyness or fear of embarrassment? You are not alone. Lots
of people are terrified of public speaking, and we all fumble
with not knowing what to say from time to time. Much advice
is available for helping you overcome this fear, but it will take
a little practice. In the meantime, if the speech paralysis takes
you by surprise, don't be afraid to take a beat or two of silence.
In that silence, call on the Holy Spirit to guide you. Take a few
rhythmic breaths and let the Holy Spirit lead.

LORD, THANK YOU FOR GIVING me the Holy Spirit,
who speaks for me when I don't know what to say in prayer.
Whether I am in front of an audience, in a small group, or
one-on-one, I can sometimes be reticent to speak up. But
You have given me things to share that others don't have, so
please give me the words and the courage to share them. In
Jesus's name I pray, amen.

Helping Our Children Renew and Rewire Their Minds

by Eryn Lynum

It's easy to pray for our children's visible needs: a scraped knee, a disappointing grade on a report card, a tear-streaked face after a friend lets them down. But how can we pray for the intangible, invisible struggles in our children's minds?

As my four children grow older, I witness their incredible mental capacities. I also struggle to know how to help them sort through their thoughts. Yet neuroscience sheds light on how God engineered our brains to create new thought patterns.

God wired our brains to be moldable. In science, this is called *neuroplasticity*, which refers to the brain's ability to change, grow, and reorganize. Scripture presents a similar concept in Romans 12:2 (NIV): "Do not conform to the pattern of this world, but be transformed by the renewing of your mind."

When my children struggle with well-worn ruts of negative thinking, I can remind them that God can reroute their thought patterns. He will help them take every thought captive and think about everything good, beautiful, and true. As they practice thinking God's thoughts, a physical remapping will occur, coinciding with a spiritual rewiring in their hearts through Jesus's redemptive power.

God designed brains—especially young brains—capable of incredible healing and reorganization. He created our children as whole beings. Their minds, spirits, and bodies work together. As we guide our children in prayer, Scripture reading, and memory, and as we take them into God's creation, they can experience physical, mental, and spiritual renewal.

Your Divine Journey

Trust in the LORD with all your heart, and do not lean on your own understanding. In all your ways acknowledge him, and he will make straight your paths.

Proverbs 3:5–6 (ESV)

Does it seem a bit of a stretch to look at your zigzagging, flawed, imperfect life so far as a divine journey? Yet it has been, and it will continue to be. By putting your life into God's hands, trusting His guidance, and leaving the outcome to Him, you can move forward with confidence and calm.

HEAVENLY FATHER, YOUR WORD SAYS that if I trust in You with all my heart, You will direct my path. When I'm not where I expected to be, remind me that if I'm walking with You, then I am in exactly the right place. Continue to guide my steps as I abide in You. I surrender my plans to You, not for Your stamp of approval but so that You can show me a better way. It's in Jesus's name that I pray, amen.

Good Change Ahead

If any of you lacks wisdom, you should ask
God, who gives generously to all without
finding fault, and it will be given to you.
James 1:5 (NIV)

Have you prayed and prayed about something and felt that
God wasn't answering you? Sometimes God uses your prayers
in unexpected ways to help you grow. Max Lucado reminds
us, "God loves us too much to indulge our every whim." If you
are struggling with feeling that God has let you down, open
your heart to Him. Let Him know you are willing to listen and
change.

DEAR LORD, I AM SO GRATEFUL THAT You are *always*
listening to me. That's why it's so hard to understand sometimes when I don't hear You. Immerse me in Your Word,
Lord. Help me to know who You are so that I trust You even
when I think You are silent. Your Word is truth, and it is
trustworthy. Help me be patient in the process. In Your name
I pray, amen.

Waiting

Wait for the LORD; be strong and take heart
and wait for the LORD.

Psalm 27:14 (NIV)

One of the roles of parenting is teaching your children that waiting is part of the process of becoming the person God wants them to be. Just as their bodies are growing and changing, waiting is a time of growth where they can experience the difference between their demands and His desires. Guide them to understand that when they surrender to His timetable, they will realize He knows best.

HEAVENLY FATHER, I LIVE IN A PLACE and time when so many things can be gained quickly, from microwaveable meals to one-hour delivery to hot water faucets. We're not used to waiting, and we've grown to not like it. As soon as a traffic light turns green, someone behind me is honking for the line to move. But You often don't move quickly, and Your timing and ways are perfect. Let Your Spirit work in my heart to bear the fruit of patience for Your perfect timing. In Jesus's name I pray, amen.

God Will Hold Your Hand

So do not fear, for I am with you; do not be dismayed, for
I am your God. I will strengthen you and help you; I will
uphold you with my righteous right hand.

Isaiah 41:10 (NIV)

In times of fear and uncertainty, the need to feel safe in God's
presence is strong. Try closing your eyes and imagining Him
taking your hand. Remember that with His support there is no
need to be afraid. He is with you, knowing the unknowns and
helping you feel secure. You are safe.

LOVING FATHER, THANK YOU for protecting me, comforting me, and guiding me through uncertain times. You
have promised to always be with me through Your Holy
Spirit, and I can trust this with all my being. There is no
place that You haven't been. If I'm walking through a dark
valley, You are with me, and You're also at the end of it. It's a
mystery of Your divine nature that I can't fully grasp but for
which I'm so thankful. You see it all, You know it all, You stay
with me through it all. I'm deeply grateful. In Jesus's name I
pray, amen.

What Really Matters

by Elsa Kok Colopy

The feeling sweeps over me on a regular basis, that sense that I've missed the boat on giving my child every opportunity to excel. Usually the feeling comes when I overhear conversations or scroll through social media and see other parents doing amazing things to train up their kids. There's one friend who has her five-year-old child enrolled in elite basketball camp. Another has taught her three-year-old how to make sushi! I look at my littles and their peanut butter and jelly masterpieces and wonder where I've gone wrong. No specialty cooking classes, no elite camps, no personalized training in the sport of their choice.

I was being particularly hard on myself one evening as I lay beside my little girl in bed. I wasn't my jovial self as she nudged me in the side. "Mama, can I see your phone?" I opened it up and handed it to her. She quickly went to the photos and started scrolling through. "That was fun, Mom!" I glanced over to see a picture of her and her brothers on the trampoline. The trampoline is located right next to our house, and as a joke, I'd thrown water out the window onto their smiling faces.

"And this, Mom. Can we do this again? Maybe next weekend?" She had found a picture of the picnic we had enjoyed with a few of her friends. I could sense God's smile as she continued to point out memories—messy, fun, and random. Maybe she won't get a scholarship to Duke for women's basketball, but my prayer is that she will have memories of moments: adventures, joy, laughter, connection, and goofiness with a family who loves her.

And that, I felt God whisper to my heart, is more than enough.

Your Life Is His Masterpiece

For we are God's masterpiece. He has created us
anew in Christ Jesus, so we can do the good things
he planned for us long ago.

Ephesians 2:10 (NLT)

God, the divine Artist, has a beautiful life planned for you.
When you offer yourself to God and dedicate yourself to be
part of His vision, you will accomplish greater things than you
can imagine. You are His masterpiece, His beloved child.

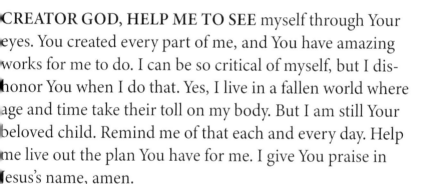

CREATOR GOD, HELP ME TO SEE myself through Your
eyes. You created every part of me, and You have amazing
works for me to do. I can be so critical of myself, but I dis-
honor You when I do that. Yes, I live in a fallen world where
age and time take their toll on my body. But I am still Your
beloved child. Remind me of that each and every day. Help
me live out the plan You have for me. I give You praise in
Jesus's name, amen.

Clear the Air

Give all your worries and cares to God, for he cares about you.

1 Peter 5:7 (NLT)

When you realize that you are being impatient with others, especially your children, remember that God understands your frustration. You can share your raw, true emotion with Him. Release whatever is bothering you. Clear the air. Often sharing the problem with Him brings greater perspective and peace.

FATHER GOD, THERE IS NOTHING You don't already know about me, so it is pointless to not share my struggles with you. When I'm sad, You collect my tears. When I'm angry, You understand. When I'm impatient, You hold my hand. Search my heart, God. Help me identify the roots of my emotions and let You help me sort them out. Keeping my cares and burdens to myself only weighs me down. Thank You for being my burden-bearer. In Jesus's name I pray, amen.

Calm Your Nerves

And the peace of God, which transcends all understanding,
will guard your hearts and your minds in Christ Jesus.
Philippians 4:7 (NIV)

We all have anxious times—moments when our nerves get the better of us. When this happens, if you can, look for a quiet place and a few quiet moments. Focus on your faith. Feel the peace of Jesus flowing over you, entering your heart and mind. Let it flood your nervous system. Replace anxious energy with His calming, soothing power.

DEAR LORD, I LONG FOR PEACE in my life. But circumstances certainly aren't going to provide peace. Only You can bring true peace. When I feel afraid, or anxious, or worried, I will seek Your face. I know that it's through prayer, with thanksgiving, that I will experience Your peace. I get caught up in trying to figure things out for myself, trying to find peace on my own. But it's truly not possible without You. Thank You for being my anchor. In Your name I pray, amen.

Time to Listen

Now choose life, so that you and your children may live and that you may love the Lord your God, listen to his voice, and hold fast to him. For the Lord is your life.
Deuteronomy 30:19–20 (NIV)

Busy people, especially moms, struggle with having enough time for a rich prayer life. When life is hectic, rather than looking for large blocks of time to spend with the Lord, take the small opportunities to pray as they come. Sometimes a few moments of quiet listening will help keep your conversation with Him going. When you listen to God's voice, He will instruct and comfort you.

HEAVENLY FATHER, YOURS IS THE dearest voice to me, because it brings me comfort, wisdom, and guidance. Just as I can recognize my child's voice when we're surrounded by other people, help me to recognize Your voice amidst the noise of my day. Remind me to take moments to be still and just be with You when I can. The fact is, I don't always have to be *doing* something. The most important thing I can do is sit with You and listen to Your words of love for me. In Jesus's name, amen.

The Unique Role of a Mother-in-Law

by Brenda L. Yoder

I had an incredible mother-in-law who impacted my life before her unexpected death. Lois was a mother of four sons and had unique relationships with her daughters-in-law. She cared for and nurtured us in ways that still influence our lives more than 20 years later.

What I appreciated about Lois was how she gently came alongside me as a young wife and mom. She assisted me with homemaking and mothering skills with kindness and understanding. She made me feel at home in her family, providing space for my uniqueness and strengths. She rarely forced her ways, opinions, or expectations on me. Instead, she invited me to help her with things that made me want to reciprocally invite her into my home or ask for her advice with questions I had.

Now as a mother-in-law and grandma, I want to model a similar relationship with my daughters-in-law. When I wonder how to approach a situation or how to build unique relationships with each of my sons' wives, I think of how I felt when Lois was present in my life. She was a welcome mentor for life skills I hadn't yet mastered. She didn't make me feel less-than or ill-equipped. Instead, she had a listening ear, compassion, and gentle suggestions.

As I've reflected on what made Lois's demeanor so inviting, I've realized she didn't try to replace or compete with my mom or present herself as the expert on motherhood. Instead, her unique role was that of mentor and friend. I try to keep this special role in the forefront of my mind with my daughters-in-law by trying not to compete with or take the place of their mothers. Instead, I'm trying to be a gentle, helpful, and welcoming presence in their lives.

Banish Self-Doubt

But let him ask in faith, with no doubting, for the
one who doubts is like a wave of the sea that is
driven and tossed by the wind.

James 1:6 (ESV)

Banish self-doubt with positivity and faith. Dr. Norman Vincent Peale said, "One of the most powerful concepts, one which is a sure cure for lack of confidence, is the thought that God is actually with you and helping you." Counteract negative thinking about what you can do through Christ who gives you strength with positive words about who God has made you to be. When doubt tries to sneak in, meet it with truth from God's Word.

DEAR GOD, WITH YOU, ALL THINGS are possible. If I have faith, I can move mountains. You have given me gifts and talents to be used for Your glory, but sometimes I can let my doubts keep me from stepping out in faith. Remind me of the power that lives within me because Your Spirit lives within me! Please don't let fear overtake me. Take my hand as You did for Peter on the Sea of Galilee and lift me above my doubts. In Jesus's name I pray, amen.

God Is Always Faithful

The steadfast love of the Lord never ceases; his mercies
never come to an end; they are new every
morning; great is your faithfulness.
Lamentations 3:22–23 (ESV)

It can feel overwhelming to live in a world where everything
is constantly changing. Life's uncertainties and unexpected
twists can sometimes make you lose your footing. When you
feel off-kilter, focus on the beautiful truth that God is always
the same. He is always and forever faithful, the same yesterday,
today, and tomorrow.

FAITHFUL LORD, YOU NEVER fail me. Everything else
around me can be changing, and You never change. You are
my steadfast rock, my fortress, my anchor in the storm. You
are my hiding place. I always know where to find You—right
by my side. Thank You for Your faithfulness. Thank You for
always keeping Your promises. I know exactly what to expect
from You: mercy, grace, and love. Thank You for never letting me go. Amen.

Childlike Faith

And he said: "Truly I tell you, unless you change
and become like little children, you will
never enter the kingdom of heaven."
Matthew 18:3 (NIV)

We spend a lot of time thinking about ways to improve what
and how we teach our children, and it is time well spent. Still,
there is so much that children can teach us, including how to
approach our God with childlike faith. Childlike faith isn't the
same as blind or unthinking faith. Instead, it is a faith that is
built on trust. It is a faith filled with wonder, curiosity, and lots of
questions. It is a faith that grows and matures over time. It is a
faith that radiates hope and joy. How can you bring elements of
a childlike faith into your own spiritual life?

FATHER, IT'S ALWAYS A JOY TO WATCH children learn
new things. When they first start reading, it opens up a
whole new world to them. That's how I want my walk with
You to be. I want to be filled with wonder and curiosity. I
want my eyes to be bright as I explore Your Word. I want
creation to teach me how to praise You wholeheartedly.
Thank You for not caring about big words and heavy theology, but just about being with me and teaching me who You
really are. In Jesus's name, amen.

Change and Resiliency

Blessed be the name of God forever and ever, to whom belong wisdom and might. He changes times and seasons; he removes kings and sets up kings; he gives wisdom to the wise and knowledge to those who have understanding; he reveals deep and hidden things; he knows what is in the darkness, and the light dwells with him.

Daniel 2:20–22 (ESV)

God's plan for our lives includes change and growth. How do you handle change? Do you create an environment for your family that strengthens resiliency? Do you encourage your children to try new things? It is important to remind yourself and your family that God pushes us beyond what we think we are capable of. He brings challenges that will guide us to become our best selves.

DEAR LORD, LIKE THE SEASONS, things around me seem to change constantly. I can't fight it or it will make me disoriented—and stressed! Please help me roll with the changes, just as creation does with the seasons. Help me to learn the lesson of the trees that have to shed their beautiful leaves in order for new growth to emerge. Teach me patience and perseverance as I walk with You through it all. You never change, and You are there when things seem dark. Help me to rely on You. In Jesus's name, amen.

Tiny Tendrils
by Peggy Frezon

Both my children were away at college, and my role as mom had changed. I was excited for their new opportunities, but I wasn't sure where I fit in. As the seasons changed, I went to my garden, my favorite place to relax and pray when I felt cast adrift by the empty nest. The flower patch thrived in part due to God's provisions of sun and rain and, I liked to believe, in part due to my tender care. This was something I could nurture, the way I used to nurture my children.

I knelt beside the rich soil and touched the tendril of a vigorous vine that had wrapped around a nearby hydrangea. Not wanting the hydrangea flower to die, I pulled the tendril away, breaking the fragile coils. The next day, I noticed that both plants had drooped and withered. *God, look what can happen when two things are separated.*

Over the following weeks, the rains came, the sun shone, and the days went by. The next time I checked on the plants, I saw that the hydrangea had filled out and grown strong and healthy. The vine also was thriving, finding new places to explore and grow. It was as if God was smiling down on me, saying, *Look what can happen when two things are separated.*

The sun warmed my face and my shoulders relaxed, knowing that my relationships with my children would always change and grow, and that God was in it all, even the empty nest stage.

Here are a few suggestions from WebMD[1] on dealing with the empty nest:

- Accept that your feelings are normal.
- Consider starting a new career, a part-time job, or a hobby.
- Volunteer for a cause you care about.

---

[1] https://www.webmd.com/parenting/how-to-manage-empty-nest-syndrome.

Stargazing

He is the Maker of the Bear and Orion, the Pleiades
and the constellations of the south.
Job 9:9 (NIV)

When was the last time you engaged in the age-old practice
of stargazing? It is a wonderful way for you and your family to
connect with the vast immensity and awesomeness of God's
creation. The darker your surroundings, the more you will see,
so you may need to travel to someplace where there is less
light pollution. Stand in the stillness and know that the One
who made the stars never changes, and your world—your
life—is held in God's perfect grasp.

CREATOR GOD, IT NEVER CEASES to amaze me that
You not only made all the stars and planets, but You know
each star by name. What we can see with our naked eyes, or
even with the most powerful telescope, is just a fraction of
the vastness of Your creation. How awesome is Your name!
Remind me each night to take a few moments and gaze at
the stars—or even at the clouds if they cover the stars—and
know that You created it all. I love You. In Jesus's name,
amen.

Forgiving Yourself

Who can discern his errors? Declare me innocent
from hidden faults.
Psalm 19:12 (ESV)

When you make a mistake, have hurt someone, or acted in a
way you shouldn't, try applying what you know about forgiving
others to yourself. Finding peace within yourself over your own
transgressions can take time, but wallowing in your own guilt
will not help. Try to repair the damage or make things right.
Give yourself grace, remembering that you are human and
mistakes happen. While it doesn't mean that you should forget
what you've done, it is important to acknowledge the wrong,
asking God and those involved for forgiveness. Then do your
best to move forward.

GOD OF NEW BEGINNINGS, I KNOW I can be hard on
myself. But locking myself in a cage of unforgiveness keeps
me from an authentic relationship with You. Keep remind-
ing me that Jesus died to forgive my sins so not forgiving
myself dishonors His sacrifice. Help me find freedom in the
grace that You have poured out upon me. Help me learn
and grow from my errors and not hold myself back from the
abundant life You have planned for me. It's in the healing
name of Jesus I pray, amen.

Take Care

Therefore, I urge you, brothers and sisters, in view of God's
mercy, to offer your bodies as a living sacrifice, holy and
pleasing to God—this is your true and proper worship.

Romans 12:1 (NIV)

As a creation of God, be sure to be a good steward of your
whole self—body, mind, and spirit. It's easy to forget that taking
care of yourself physically is an important aspect of your faith.
And, of course, setting a good-health example for your children
is important. Getting enough sleep, eating well, and exercising
all play a part in living your best life and aligning yourself with
God's plan.

HEAVENLY FATHER, THANK YOU FOR making my body
so extraordinary. The way all the systems work together is
truly amazing. And You have given me stewardship over this
gift. It is mine alone to care for. Please help me take the time
to exercise, to be still and quiet with You, and to eat healthy
foods. Please help me become wise about my sleep habits,
including the time I go to bed. Guide me to set a good example for the younger people in my life. Thank You for walking
with me. In Jesus's name, amen.

Courage and Strength

> "Be strong and of good courage, do not fear nor be
> afraid of them; for the LORD your God, He is the One who
> goes with you. He will not leave you nor forsake you."
> *Deuteronomy 31:6 (NKJV)*

There will be hard times when you need courage to keep going. Tap into the Source of courage by feeling God's presence.
Hear Him say, "I am with you always." Pray for courage, and He
will help you move beyond your fear. Pray for strength, and He
will help you find your inner fortitude.

DEAR LORD, THE POWER OF YOUR presence is always
with me, right here in my heart, giving me the courage
to face anything. You are the same God who brought the
Israelites out of slavery in Egypt. You parted the Red Sea.
You gave Mary the courage to carry the Messiah. You gave
the disciples courage to spread the gospel in sometimes
hostile places. You are the same God now. You can help me
face anything. I am so grateful that You never leave me. Even
if I'm afraid of small things, You never let me go. Thank You.
In Jesus's name, amen.

Modeling a More Positive Perspective

by Janet Holm McHenry

I got caught in a prayer one day.

It all started when I was prepping dinner for unexpected company. Some out-of-state friends had called to say they would stop by on their way through the area, so I invited them to dinner.

My youngest, Bethany, six, was helping me by setting the table and fetching me utensils and other items. Apparently, she was also listening to me grumbling about my hard day at work, last-minute company, and the messy house I had to clean.

When it was time for grace at dinner, I was too tired to come up with the right words, so I said, "Who'd like to pray?"

"I will," Bethany quickly responded. "Oh, Lord, why did these people have to come to dinner tonight? They made Mommy grumpy. But bless the food anyway. Amen."

This taught me a lesson about holding my tongue in front of children, but it also taught me that I could model a more prayerful and positive perspective—one that teaches trust in God through life's challenges. Here are some simple prayers to say aloud with our children:

- Finances: "God, You have always provided for us, so I know You will meet every need."
- Illness: "Lord, You healed many people in the Bible, so we ask You for Your healing touch."
- Bullying: "Father, we ask You for good friends who will stand by us on good days and bad days."
- Injustice: "God, we know that sometimes life isn't fair. We trust You for all the details of this hard situation."
- Contentment: "Thank You, God, for making me who I am. Thank You also for the life and people and things You have given me. I appreciate all that I have."

Little Things

"His master said to him, 'Well done, good and faithful servant. You have been faithful over a little; I will set you over much. Enter into the joy of your master.'"

Matthew 25:21 (ESV)

The parable of the good and faithful servant stresses the value of little things. Sometimes when it comes to our faith, we think in larger-than-life terms. We think that grand gestures are how we can show the depth of our faith. But this parable reminds us that it is the little things we do that cause us to "enter into the joy of the Master."

DEAR LORD, THANK YOU FOR NOT requiring that I earn Your favor. My works are not what save me. But when I take the things You have entrusted to me and use them for Your glory, I know that You are pleased. Help me to understand that big things are all well and good, but when I am faithful in the little ways, it makes a big difference. Especially to those little eyes that are watching. Thank You for giving me so many gifts. Help me to steward them well. In Jesus's name I pray, amen.

God's Perfect Love

Jesus replied: "Love the Lord your God with all your
heart and with all your soul and with all your mind."
Matthew 22:37 (NIV)

Loving God is a process that begins with consistently spending
time with Him. When you don't have large blocks of time, small
moments with Him matter. As you grow your relationship with
Him, you become open to His ways, and your priorities fall into
place. Most important, you show your love for Him by sharing
His love with others—especially your children.

DEAR LORD, I LONG TO LOVE YOU with every fiber
of my being. Long, quiet stretches of time with You are
wonderful, but so are the shorter moments. Sometimes
just a whispered prayer, a short recitation of a psalm, or
a moment of silence to hear Your voice refreshes my soul.
When I acknowledge Your presence in every moment of my
day, I feel at peace. When I see Your handiwork in nature, I
know that You are able to do all things. Thank You for every
moment that I can carve out with You. They add up to quality time. In Jesus's name I pray, amen.

Hope

For in this hope we were saved. Now hope that is seen
is no hope at all. For who hopes for what he sees?

Romans 8:24 (ESV)

No matter what problems you face, it's important to keep hope
alive in your life and to reflect that hope to your family and
friends. Hope is a great renewing force. Whenever difficulties
and trouble come upon you, ask God to reassure you that
things will get better.

FATHER, YOU ARE MY REFUGE and strength. Brighten
my dark thoughts and fill me with hope. Remind me that
You are always there with me, and that You already know
what the future holds. I have a choice to make: Will I trust
You or not? If You are good—and I know that You are—then
You are good even in the dark times. Let Your light of hope
shine into that darkness. Help me remember that forever is
longer than this. In Jesus's name I pray, amen.

Worldly Problems

"Therefore I tell you, do not worry about your life,
what you will eat or drink; or about your body,
what you will wear. Is not life more than food,
and the body more than clothes?"

Matthew 6:25 (NIV)

On stressful days you may feel as if no one understands what you're going through. Try not to fret over inconsequential things. For the larger worries, remind yourself that you are not alone. Jesus said to take heart. His presence helps you overcome worldly problems that weigh you down. His glorious victory can change and transform every moment of your life.

HEAVENLY FATHER, HELP ME TO TAKE You at Your word. You said that You will provide what I need. You said that You will always be with me. You said to cast my cares upon You because You care for me. Those are wonderful promises, and You *always* keep Your promises. I know I have nothing to fear, and worrying adds nothing to my life. Thank You for Your faithfulness to me. It's in the matchless name of Jesus I pray, amen.

Mothers of the Bible

by Lisa Guernsey

*For you created my inmost being; you knit me
together in my mother's womb.*
Psalm 139:13 (NIV)

What can the mothers of the Bible tell us? They may be thousands of years removed from us, but their lives still resonate. In fact, the Bible is rich with the stories of women who anchored their families—spiritually as well as physically—often against long odds.

When we think of those moms, our mind instantly leaps to the New Testament and to the life of Mary, the mother of Jesus. The Gospel of Luke tells us of Mary's encounter with the angel Gabriel. When the angel foretells Jesus's conception through the Holy Spirit, Mary replies, "I am the Lord's servant.... May your word to me be fulfilled" (Luke 1:38, NIV). Her answer, full of faith and humility, begins her journey as a mother, one that would be marked by extremes of joy and grief.

The same chapter of Luke references another recipient of divine aid: Mary's much older cousin Elizabeth. "The Lord has done this for me," she says of her pregnancy in old age (Luke 1:25, NIV). Elizabeth's son, John the Baptist, would later prove pivotal in the life of Jesus. The Old Testament references similar miracle conceptions, including those of Sarah, mother of Isaac (Genesis 17, 21), and Hannah, mother of the prophet Samuel (1 Samuel 1), who hands over her son to the priest Eli, dedicating her son to the Lord's service.

An angel also appears to the childless mother of Samson. As with the angel Gabriel to Mary, he gives her insight into her child's future: "You will become pregnant and have a son whose head is never to be touched by a razor because the boy is to be a Nazirite, dedicated to God from the womb. He will take the lead in delivering Israel from the hands of the Philistines" (Judges 13:5, NIV). A search of the Bible finds many more such instances of motherhood after infertility, including Rebekah, mother of Esau and Jacob (Genesis 25:21), and Rachel, mother of Joseph and Benjamin (Genesis 30:22).

Other women, like Mary, endure terrible hardship over the course of their motherhoods. Eve, the first mother, sees one son murder the other out of jealousy (Genesis 4). Cast out of her home, Hagar despairs that her son, Ishmael, will perish in the desert (Genesis 21:15–16). Jochebed, the enslaved mother of Moses, floats her infant in a basket in the Nile (Exodus 2), balancing the dangers of the crocodile-filled river against the certainty of the newborn's death by the Egyptian pharaoh's decree.

What else did these women have in common? Each mother continued to be under God's watch and care. Eve is ultimately consoled by the birth of her third son, Seth. Hagar not only discovers, with God's help, a well of water that will save Ishmael but is told he will found "a great nation" (Genesis 21:18, NIV). And we all know the story of how the baby Moses is rescued from the river and grows up under the protection of the pharaoh's daughter. As an adult, Moses becomes the great leader who rescues the Jews from centuries of enslavement and hands down God's Ten Commandments to us.

The influence of mothers on the raising of their children is also seen throughout the Bible. Though unnamed, the mother of King Lemuel gives us a good example. Along with her memorable notes on a "wife of noble character...She is worth far more than rubies" (Proverbs 31:10), she gave her son advice for living and ruling, preserved for us over the ages. Among her wise and temperate words is this plea to look after the less fortunate:

Speak up for those who cannot speak for themselves,
for the rights of all who are destitute.
Speak up and judge fairly;
defend the rights of the poor and needy.
—Proverbs 31:8–9 (NIV)

How like a mom to advocate for those who need protection!

Some of the Bible's most memorable mothers are mothers by choice, not by birth. After her husband and two sons die in a new land, Naomi urges her daughters-in-law to return to their local families. One of the women tearfully departs, but the other, Ruth, refuses, vowing to remain with Naomi (Ruth 1). Bound by love of each other and of God, they return to Naomi's homeland to face challenges and, working as a unit, succeed in building a new life and family there.

Each of these women's lives, spanning the millennia of the Bible, continues to be instructive today: Mothers—and thus the children they raise—are to be full of faith, to trust in God, to love. May we moms of today see their paths renewed and laid out for us so that we can follow in their footsteps.

Our Contributors

Jeannie Blackmer is an author who lives in Boulder, Colorado, with her husband, Zane, and their chocolate lab, Ody. Her most recent books include *Talking to Jesus: A Fresh Perspective on Prayer* and *Mom-Sense: A Common Sense Guide to Confident Mothering*. She has been a freelance writer for more than 30 years and has worked in the publishing industry with a variety of authors on more than twenty-five books, most recently writing content for The MomCo, a global ministry to moms. She's passionate about using written words to inspire hope in women and encourage growth in their relationships with Jesus. She loves chocolate (probably too much), scuba diving, beekeeping, a good inspirational story, her family, and being outside as much as possible. Maintaining a sense of humor has helped save her sanity as she now navigates the fun and challenges of relationships with three very adventurous adult sons, one amazing daughter-in-law, three wild grand-dogs, and a colorful, kind of creepy chameleon. Find out more about Jeannie on her website at jeannieblackmer.com. *See pages 15, 65, 85*.

Elsa Kok Colopy is an author, speaker, and expert on multiple DVD curriculums (Single & Parenting, Griefshare, Surviving the Holidays, DivorceCare). A former editor for *Thriving Family* magazine, Elsa has authored hundreds of articles and is the author of six books, including *Pure Love Pure Life: Exploring God's Heart on Purity* (Zondervan); *A Woman Who Hurts, A God Who Heals* (New Hope); *A Woman with a Past, a God with a Future* (New Hope); and *99 Ways to Fight Worry and Stress* (Navigators). A former single parent, Elsa has now been married to Brian for 18 years. Together they are the proud parents of four adult children and four adopted littles (three from Haiti, one adopted domestically). *See pages 30, 45, 110.*

Courtney Ellis is a pastor, speaker, and the author of five books, including *Looking Up: A Birder's Guide to Hope Through Grief* (IVP). She also hosts *The Thing with Feathers* podcast, a show about birds and hope. She lives in Southern California with her husband, Daryl, and their three children. *See pages 20, 50.*

Peggy Frezon, a contributing editor of *Guideposts* and *Angels on Earth* magazines, is a proud mom and grandma to five redheads. Peggy grew up in Vermont with dogs, cats, rabbits, guinea pigs, gerbils, and turtles, and was caregiver to any animal that followed her home. She frequently writes about her favorite topic—the human-animal bond—and is the author of several books about dogs and the people who love them. She's also co-author of *Mini Horse, Mighty Hope* (Revell). Peggy is a regular contributor to *All God's Creatures Daily Devotions for Animal Lovers* and has contributed to *Pray a Word a Day* and other devotionals. She and her husband, Mike, have two rescue guinea pigs and rescue golden retrievers at BrooksHaven, their *furever* retirement home for senior dogs. Reflecting on her rescue work, she says, "I learned that it's not always about what a dog can do for me, but what I can do for that dog." Connect with Peggy at peggyfrezon.com and keep up to date with dog and book news with her newsletter *Dogs of BrooksHaven* at https://tinyurl.com/BrooksHaven. *See pages 25, 60, 75, 120.*

Lisa Guernsey is Copy Lead for *Guideposts* magazine, which she well remembers from her grandmother's house in Upstate New York. Her grandmother also set her on a journey of faith, encouraging her to read a children's Bible all the way through as a child. Now living in New York City, Lisa and her husband, Nick, enjoy the challenges (and awesome privilege) of raising two boys. You can often find Lisa at her local community garden, where she is ever so slowly developing a green thumb while putting together programs of special events for the community, or nose-deep in a book on the American Revolutionary War. Though she mostly uses the red pen of a copy editor, she relishes those writing opportunities that come her way. Her articles have appeared on Guideposts.org and in *CT Explored*. **See Introduction and page 131.**

Julie Lavender is a woman of many hats, including journalist, author, speaker, former teacher, former homeschooling mom, and wife to her high school and college sweetheart, David, but her favorite hat of all is mommy. Those four, previously homeschooled students, two girls and two boys, are now college-graduated adults living farther away than Julie would like. She enjoyed welcoming two sons-in-love into the family, as well as a precious grandson five years ago. Julie loved being a military wife for 20 years while David served in the Navy. Her family lived in nine homes in six states before retiring from the military and settling back in their hometown of Statesboro, Georgia.

Julie is the author of *Children's Bible Stories for Bedtime*; *Strength for All Seasons: A Mom's Devotional of Powerful Verses and Prayers*; and *365 Ways to Love Your Child: Turning Little Moments into Lasting Memories*. She looks forward to two picture books and four children's educational books, which she co-authored with her husband, coming out in the next 2 years. **See page 100.**

Eryn Lynum is a certified master naturalist, educator, national speaker, and author of *Rooted in Wonder: Nurturing Your Family's Faith Through God's Creation* and *936 Pennies: Discovering the Joy of Intentional Parenting*. Eryn hosts the popular podcast for kids, *Nat Theo: Nature Lessons Rooted in the Bible*. She lives in northern Colorado with her husband, Grayson, and their four children, whom they homeschool. Eryn teaches natural theology—what we learn about God through what He has created, from Romans 1:20. She teaches using materials in creation to communicate biblical truth in memorable ways. Eryn enjoys leading community nature hikes and programs. Sometimes she even brings her pet axolotl, Spud, to teach about regeneration and how God renews our minds and hearts. She's an avid birdwatcher thanks to the inspiration of her husband and son. Eryn has been featured on broadcasts including Focus on the Family, FamilyLife Today, Christian Parenting, and Raising Christian Kids. Every opportunity she gets, she is out exploring God's creation with her family and sharing her adventures at erynlynum.com. *See pages 10, 55, 80, 105.*

Janet Holm McHenry's best moments are those spent with her cattle rancher husband, Craig, and their four adult children. A national speaker, Janet is an award-winning author of twenty-six books—seven on prayer, including the bestselling *PrayerWalk, The Complete Guide to the Prayers of Jesus,* and her newest, *Praying Personalities: Finding Your Natural Prayer Style.* She serves on the California leadership team for the National Day of Prayer, as county coordinator for Pray California, and as the prayer ministries coordinator of The Bridge Church in Reno for the last 20 years. Janet's prayer-walking practices have been featured in radio, television, and podcast programs, as well as in magazines such as *Health, Family Circle,* and *First for Women.* She is the creator of an online Teachable course called Prayer School, a certified life coach and personalities trainer, and the host of the Sierra Valley Writers Retreat. A journalism graduate of UC Berkeley, Janet formerly worked as a newspaper journalist and high school English teacher. In fact, she taught English to all her children at least one year in their small, rural school...and somehow they all survived! *See pages 40, 95, 125.*

Brenda L. Yoder is a licensed mental health counselor, elementary school counselor, speaker, former teacher, and author of *Uncomplicated: Simple Secrets for a Compelling Life; Fledge: Launching Your Kids Without Losing Your Mind;* and *Balance, Busyness, and Not Doing It All.* She has been featured in Guideposts' *Mornings with Jesus* devotionals; *Chicken Soup for the Soul* books; and *The Washington Post.* She hosts the *Midlife Moms* and *Life Beyond the Picket Fence* podcasts and the Midlife Moms Facebook Group. Brenda twice won the Touchstone Award for teachers.

Brenda is a former history teacher and lover of antiques, gardens, front porch rockers, and her grandkids. She and her husband, Ron, raised four children on their family dairy farm in northern Indiana, where they currently raise Bernese Mountain dogs, goats, chickens, and cattle and host an Airbnb. They love camping and visiting their grandchildren and adult children throughout the country. Brenda loves gardening, decorating, and having good conversations over coffee. You can connect with her on Instagram or at brendayoder.com, where she writes about life, faith, and family beyond the storybook image. *See pages 35, 70, 90, 115.*

Entries by Theme

Comfort 16, 24, 28, 37, 61, 62, 68, 76, 84, 89, 103, 113, 122, 123
Courage 39, 51, 66, 72, 82, 104, 109, 116
Faith 14, 21, 23, 31, 49, 56, 57, 63, 69, 78, 83, 99, 117, 126
Hearing God 9, 18, 42, 53, 58, 64, 71, 101, 107, 114
Hope 6, 19, 27, 38, 54, 77, 97, 128
Joy 22, 26, 29, 33, 43, 44, 67, 81, 88, 93, 118
Self-control 8, 32, 36, 41, 92, 112
Strength 7, 34, 47, 52, 87, 102, 119, 124
Trust 11, 12, 17, 46, 48, 73, 74, 91, 94, 96, 98, 108, 129
Wisdom 13, 59, 79, 86, 106, 111, 121, 127

A Note from the Editors

We hope you enjoyed *A Moment for Mom: Everyday Devotions and Prayers,* published by Guideposts. For over 75 years, Guideposts, a nonprofit organization, has been driven by a vision of a world filled with hope. We aspire to be the voice of a trusted friend, a friend who makes you feel more hopeful and connected.

By making a purchase from Guideposts, you join our community in touching millions of lives, inspiring them to believe that all things are possible through faith, hope, and prayer. Your continued support allows us to provide uplifting resources to those in need. Whether through our communities, websites, apps, or publications, we inspire our audiences, bring them together, and comfort, uplift, entertain, and guide them. Visit us at guideposts.org to learn more.

We would love to hear from you. Write us at Guideposts, P.O. Box 5815, Harlan, Iowa 51593 or call us at (800) 932-2145. Did you love *A Moment for Mom*? Please leave a review for this product on guideposts.org/shop. Your feedback helps others in our community find relevant products.

Find inspiration, find faith, find Guideposts.
Shop our best sellers and favorites at
guideposts.org/shop

Or scan the QR code to go directly to our Shop

Made in United States
North Haven, CT
03 May 2024

52071647R10078